Children's Ministries

IDEAS AND TECHNIQUES THAT WORK

A HANDBOOK FOR CHILDREN'S MINISTRIES

Advent*Source*

Copyright © 1997 by the Church Resource Consortium
North American Division

Revised 2006

Publisher: Advent*Source*
Project Manager: Cherie Skrivan
Editor: Ann Calkins
Contributors: Eugene Brewer, Debra Brill, Steve Case, Fred Cornforth, Debee Givens, Cheryl Woolsey Holloway, Polly Johnson, Noelene Johnsson, Barbara Manspeaker, Suzanne Perdew, Jim Pierson, Margaret Taglavore
Copy Editor: Joyce Jesse

Designer: Steve Trapero

To order additional copies:
Advent*Source*
5040 Prescott Avenue
Lincoln, NE 68506
1-800-328-0525

No part of this publication may be reproduced, stored in a retrieval system, or transmitted, in any form or by any means, electronic, photocopying, recording, or otherwise, without prior written permission.

Publication Data
Children's ministries: ideas and techniques that work/ edited by Ann M. Calkins. Advent*Source*, 1997. 174 p.
Includes bibliographical references.
    ISBN 1-57756-005-1
    1. Church work with children.
    2. Christian education of children.

Printed in the United States of America.

Foreword

The Seventh-day Adventist Church has a long history of ministry to children. We take seriously Christ's injunctions to "suffer the little children to come." Ellen White, one of the church's founders, wrote long ago that "part of the work of parents and of Christ's ambassadors (is) to see that the children are properly instructed in the Word of God."

Anyone who has volunteered to teach children in church can testify that doing so is no easy matter. One must first secure the attention of the children. Then one must speak at their level, keeping their attention. And that is a problem. We almost need to learn four or five different languages—one for each stage of a child's development. But to connect with a child, voila, what delight! There is truly no nicer ministry than children's ministry—no greater delight than to see the sparkle that lights a child's eyes when his mind opens to the Son of Righteousness.

Childhood today is as dangerous as a minefield. More than ever, children need a caring and understanding experience at church to steady their minds for spiritual learning. They need a helping hand and lots of loving encouragement as they start their life's journey. They need someone to teach them to read the map that will guide them safely through the dangerous terrain. They need someone like you.

The purpose of *Children's Ministries: Ideas and Techniques That Work* is to share the expertise of those who have been successful spiritual guides to children. These ministries specialists tell about the ages and stages of childhood and how to teach children at each level. They describe today's children and present creative ways to lead them to Jesus.

Noelene Johnsson
Noelene Johnsson
Children's Ministries Director
North American Division

Table of Contents

Using This Book — 1
Introduction — 3
Chapter 1: The Mission of Children's Ministries — 5
    Mission Statement
    A Shared Vision
    Understanding Our Mission Statement
    Developing Relational Ministries
    Understanding Grace-Oriented Ministries
    Developing Inclusive Ministries
    Ways to Practice an Inclusive Ministry
    Developing Informed Ministries
    Other Educational Opportunities
    Professional Ministries Networks
    Cooperative Ministries

Chapter 2: The Ages and Stages of Childhood — 21
    Today's Child
    Children Then and Now
    Basic Needs of Children
    The Beginner Child
    The Kindergarten Child
    The Primary Child
    The Junior Student
    The Earliteen Student

Chapter 3: Leading a Child to Jesus — 37
    Five Imperatives for Committed Children and Youth
    Leading a Child to Christ
    Helping Children Grow in Jesus

Chapter 4: Faith Development and the Life Stages — 43
    Defining Faith
    How Children Think

Chapter 5: Learning Styles   **57**
    Know Your Style
    The Four Learning Styles
    Learning Styles—So What?

Chapter 6: Modes of Learning   **65**
    Understanding the Modes
    Planning Multi-sensory, Active Learning for All Modes

Chapter 7: Understanding Active Learning   **77**
    Children Remember What They Do
    The Discovery Style Lesson
    How to Make Active Learning Work
    Bible Learning Activities
    Using Bible Learning Activities
    Readiness Activities
    Application Activities
    Types of Bible Learning Activities
    Bible Learning Centers

Chapter 8: Organizing Your Ministry Program   **89**
    Developing a Children's Ministries Plan
    Look at the Big Picture
    Overall Plan
    Resource Your Ministry Plan
    Publicize Your Ministry
    Work Your Plan
    Plan for Succession

Chapter 9: Children's Ministries Programs & Job Descriptions   **105**

Chapter 10: Understanding Children with Special Needs   **121**
    Becoming Advocates for Children with Special Needs
    Making Your Ministry Inclusive
    Physical Disabilities
    Mission Statement
    Blindness/Visual Impairment
    Deafness/Hearing Impairments
    Learning Disabilities
    Attention Deficit Disorder
    Emotional Disorders

Children with Mental Impairment
Children Coping with Loss
Children from Single-Parent Homes
Ministering to Children Who Have Been Abused
Physical Abuse
Sexual Abuse

Chapter 11: Positive Discipline   **139**
Styles of Discipline
Why Discipline Breaks Down
Prevention, The Best Cure
Planning for Success
Preventing Disruptions
Instant Attention Getters
Emotionally Safe Classrooms
Friendly Classrooms
Self-discipline in the Classroom
Noise, Reverence and Learning
Disruption Stoppers for Active Learners
Emergency Measures
Taking Responsibility
Questions Teachers Most Often Ask

Chapter 12: Staffing Children's Ministries   **155**
Laying a Foundation for Volunteer Ministries
Nurturing Volunteers
Communicating with Volunteers
Training Volunteers
Reasons to Meet With Volunteers
Planning Meetings for Volunteers
Basics for Successful Meetings
Showing That You Care
Recruiting Volunteers

Appendix A: Where to Order Materials   **169**
Appendix B: Planning a Children's Ministry Budget   **171**
Recommended Resources   **173**

Using This Book

Children's Ministries: Ideas and Techniques That Work, designed for busy coordinators, leaders, and volunteers, is easy to read and user-friendly.

Need some information about learning styles? Want a list of Children's Ministries job descriptions? Chapters can be "mixed and matched"—customized to fit the learning needs of your local Children's Ministries team.

You'll also want to "Try This" or introduce your children to a creative "Great Idea!" Here's what it's all about…

"Try This" An idea or activity designed to motivate or educate your adult team members.

"Great Idea!" Ideas to enliven and involve children in creative spiritual learning.

Rule of Thumb A common sense strategy for working with children.

Conventional Wisdom "Words to the wise" from children's ministry specialists.

Introduction

Imagine, for a moment, a hillside in Galilee. We've been toiling up the rocky path and we've almost reached the great Teacher. We're anticipating an afternoon listening to His stories. Down the path toward us comes a mother, sagging with embarrassment. She tugs at a child who, feet dragging and shoulders twisting, looks back up the hill.

"Why doesn't Jesus want to see us, Mama?" the child asks.

The mother tries to hush the child without wounding her sensitive heart. If this mother in Israel were given the opportunity to shrivel up and disappear, she would take it without question.

Unnoticed by the departing pair, Jesus courteously disengages Himself from the knot of men in deep discussion around Him. In a few strides He reaches the mother and child. Smiling down at the little girl, He reaches for her hand.

"I want to see you," He says. "I'm always glad to see you. And, in a voice which rings across the hillside and down through the ages, He says, "Let the children come to me. Don't do anything that would keep them away."

How tenderly He draws each child's heart close to His own. He has charms that even the very littlest ones recognize and eagerly respond to. If they but get a chance to see Him.

And that is our challenge. To let the children we work with really see Jesus. As we plan our Children's Ministries programs and meetings, that is our most humbling challenge. Can the children see Jesus?

Children's Ministries: Ideas & Techniques that Work will help you answer this question and give you the tools to plan an effective Children's Ministries program.

1 The Mission of Children's Ministries

Mission Statement

The mission of Children's Ministries' leaders and teachers is to reach out to children and draw them into a loving, productive and lasting relationship with Jesus Christ and with their church and to train, resource, and support those who minister to children.

A Shared Vision for Children's Ministries

The goal of Children's Ministries is to empower and resource those at every level who engage in ministry to children so as to develop:

1. **Relational ministries**, in which volunteers understand children and help them form a lasting friendship with Jesus that is based on the gospel elements of grace, worship, community and service.
2. **Inclusive ministries**, in which both the volunteers who minister and the children to whom they minister will be valued and involved, regardless of race, skin color, language, gender, age, or socio-economic circumstances.

3. **Informed ministries**, so that trained personnel, understanding the mission and methods and having the resources for effective ministry, mobilize for children's outreach and nurture.
4. **Professional ministries networks** empower those who minister to children to encourage, inform, train, and empower others for effective ministry to children.
5. **Cooperative ministries** join with other ministries, such as family, youth, Pathfinder, and pastoral ministries, as well as ADRA and Adventist Community Services, for wider ministry and service.

Understanding Our Mission Statement

The mission statement for Children's Ministries is best understood in the context of the great Commission in Matthew 28:19-20: "Therefore go and make disciples of all nations, baptizing them in the name of the Father and of the Son and of the Holy Spirit, and teaching them to obey everything I have commanded you" (NIV).

Children's Ministries recognizes that making disciples of children is a specialized work because children are special people. They have special needs and speak a special level of language, and have their own special perspective on life, love, and learning.

Note that, while it is easy enough to baptize children and teach them to obey (at least, temporarily), this is not the goal of Children's Ministries or of the great commission. Making disciples is the goal. Of course, discipleship results in baptism and obedience.

In eastern countries today there are still disciples who follow their teacher, usually a "holy" man, everywhere he goes. Not only is the disciple learning from the master teacher in all the verbal exchanges that occur in a given day, but the disciple also observes the teacher's interactions and experiences the teacher's life. A disciple is bound to the teacher by these experiences and eventually may become quite like the teacher in mannerisms and thinking.

A disciple of long standing eventually becomes a teacher in his own right and may have disciples of his own.

Spiritual teachers in the church are called to model discipleship. However, they encourage young Christians to become disciples of Jesus. The Christian discipling process is meant to come full circle; the new disciple brings someone else to follow Jesus. Thus, nurturing children into "a loving and productive relationship with Jesus Christ" means discipling them to the extent that they lead others to Jesus.

"Everyone who is fully trained will be like his teacher."
—Luke 6:40 (NIV)

Just as Jesus did not confine His ministry to His disciples, so Children's Ministries is not to confine itself to the children of the church. God wants us to look out for the needs of all children. As we help to meet the temporal needs of children in our communities, earning their trust and friendship, we earn the right to talk to them of spiritual things as Jesus did in His day.

"Christ's method alone will give true success in reaching the people. The Savior mingled with men as one who desired their good. He showed His sympathy for them, ministered to their needs, and won their confidence. Then He bade them, 'Follow Me.'"
—Ellen G. White, Ministry of Healing, page 143.

In addition to being actively involved in the community, every disciple of Jesus Christ is given a mandate to be involved in mission to the world. And just as ministry to children in the church needs to be specialized, so the church needs to probe the special needs of children in the countries and people groups that our global mission targets. Children's Ministries leaders and teachers need to expand their global vision.

But for Children's Ministries, mission consciousness is not meant to be so broad as to be staggering. Jesus came to fulfill His mission at a low point in human history. Children enjoyed no rights; most were denied the kind of diet and education that Jesus knew to be desirable. Unbelieving adults often stood in the way of His ministry.

But Jesus did not let these depressing odds paralyze His ministry. He went about ministry, one day at a time, one person at a time.

My son rarely talks about India, the country of his birth. He says, "I just remember the awful poverty and knowing that I couldn't do anything about it." Somehow we had failed to reassure him that his friendship, smiles, and sharing food and his books and toys all helped—one person at a time. Teachers likewise are accomplishing Christ's commission when they invite one child at a time to accept Jesus.

—Noelene Johnsson

Developing Relational Ministries

A right relationship with God is the goal of Christian ministry and of salvation; Christ's style of ministry was relational. Relational ministries put a high priority on people, without sacrificing message. Relational Children's Ministries build friendships with children, helping them make friends with Jesus.

"Ministry is developed around relationships. If you don't have the relationship, you don't do the ministry."

—Ron Whitehead

Relational ministries consider the children, their development, and their needs ahead of the knowledge that we want to teach them. But that does not mean that teaching Bible truth does not matter. We need to: (1) understand children: (2) understand the message (Bible truth): and (3) understand how to deliver the message so as to make it appealing and understandable to children.

How Relational Is My Ministry?

An Informal Personal Assessment for Leaders

Directions: For each statement, choose the response that is most typical of you.

1. When my program is about to start, you will most likely find me
   - **a.** Finalizing my plans or materials
   - **b.** Welcoming the children

2. Most of the time spent in preparation is devoted to
   - **a.** Preparing visual aids
   - **b.** Meeting the needs of the children

3. I evaluate my success with a program in terms of
   - **a.** Keeping the kids' interest
   - **b.** Meeting kids' needs

4. For me, the main purpose of a lesson or program is to
   - **a.** Teach Bible knowledge
   - **b.** Help kids better know and love God

5. When I teach I am more conscious of
   - **a.** The content of the Bible lesson
   - **b.** How God can help kids solve their problems.

6. I know my students by name.
   - **a.** No
   - **b.** Yes

7. I have visited with my students in their family setting.
   - **a.** No
   - **b.** Yes

8. My first concern with a new class is
   - **a.** Getting them to respect me
   - **b.** Getting to know each student

9. I most want the room in which I teach to look
   - **a.** Organized and neat
   - **b.** Student-friendly

10. I am involved in Children's Ministries because
    - **a.** I love teaching
    - **b.** I love kids

SCORING:
The "b" responses indicate a relational orientation:
- 8-10 "b" responses — great relational orientation
- 5-7 "b" responses — good relational orientation
- Less than 5 "b" responses — lots of room to grow into a relational ministry!

Understanding Grace-Oriented Ministries

The gospel elements of grace, worship, community, and service make a relational ministry particularly appealing and fruitful for the kingdom of God. Grace emphasizes the God →child relationship and paves the way for the child →God (worship), child → believers (community), and child →world (service) responses.

Try This...

Relational Ministry Tips for Teachers
- Help the children to feel comfortable with each other. Warm the class atmosphere so it is cheerful and friendly. Smile a lot. Be open, accepting, and affirming of all. Model an out-going interest in individuals.

- At every opportunity verbalize your feelings in a friendly way.
  "I feel safe sharing this with you because I know you won't laugh at me."
  "I like you because you say how you feel."
  "Let's continue to respect each other's opinions."
  "I like the way you said that. I think I understand what you mean."

- Give friendly messages:
  "We like kids in our church."
  "At our church we take good care of shy people."
  "Kids like being in our class because we are friendly and kind."

- Learn all you can about the age level you are teaching. Try to keep up with their interests, fads and favorites. Note what bothers them and what scares them. What do they lie awake worrying about? Plan your Bible lessons so as to bring answers to their deepest questions and reassure their hidden fears.

- Choose curriculum materials with an approach to Bible study that is appropriate to a relational ministry and to the child's developmental level.

A Christ-centered, grace-oriented ministry can be modeled after Christ's example. Jesus did not just tell people about God's love, He became their Friend—He loved them. And Jesus did not just talk about grace, He modeled grace—forgiveness, unconditional love, and complete acceptance for all. And in the ultimate demonstration of grace, He died a death He did not deserve so that we can have the gift of eternal life that we do not deserve. Grace, undeserved favor, is the basis of both our relationship to God and of our ministry to children.

Our whole life is a response to grace. Every Bible story we tell, every song we sing, even our obedience, is a response to grace. Either we are indifferent to grace or we celebrate it as an act of worship. Our ministry to children is a loving response to grace, rising like sweet incense offered to God.

An understanding of grace and an appreciation of Jesus our Lord also draws us into a special relationship with others in the community of faith, and compels us to reach out in acts of service both within the community of believers and beyond to the unsaved world around us.

What possibilities if we will work in partnership with Jesus, empowered by the Holy Spirit, to let grace saturate our relationships with children! Leading them to Jesus becomes our highest priority.

Protecting children from harsh criticism, encouraging them to bloom in the garden of God, teaching them how to grow strong in

Try This...

Ways to Make Ministry Grace-Oriented

- **Make grace the basic message** and model for every lesson and program. After all, grace is central to the story of the great controversy between Christ and Satan. So when telling a Bible story, give the kids a perspective of how grace relates to the story. For instance, tell the story of David and Goliath from the perspective of the forces of evil about to prevail and God using one seemingly insignificant person to ensure freedom (salvation) for all.

- **Make grace the motivating force** in your lessons and admonitions. As children grow older and begin to challenge the boundaries of authority, they sometimes shock us with their attitudes and behavior. Instead of scaring them into submission (You won't go to heaven if you don't conform/perform.) or humiliating them with guilt (Think of your influence. What will people think of the church? We don't want to make Jesus sad. What if Jesus comes and your sin isn't forgiven?), appeal to them with love as a motivator (Isn't God great? don't you just love Him? How might you show you love Him this week?)

- **Choose curriculum materials that are based on the gospel elements**—grace, worship, community, and service. Many programs tend to stress behavior as a goal instead of as a response to grace.

- **Value and model grace** in the classroom. To have a grace-oriented ministry, we must be saturated with grace ourselves. People tend to talk about things they truly value. If we value Jesus, we will give Him prime time in our conversation. So let's think more intentionally about what it means to be Christ-like and then ask Him to make us like that, transforming us from the inside out.

- **Teach children to listen to God and respond to grace**. Teach children to figure out what God might be trying to tell them through a Bible story. If we impose our application of the story, we are likely to get into something that they are not ready for. If we ask them what the story says to them, they will likely be right on target.

- **Personally grow in grace**. Look and listen for information that gives you insight into grace and that inspires your continued response to it. Look for new ways to give children messages of grace.

Six Activities that Teach Grace

1. **Noah and the ark.** Use a large appliance box as the ark when you tell this Bible story. Let the children act the part of Noah's family or the animals. Hug them as they respond to the invitation to come into the ark. Tell them about the only God who had a plan to save all His people.

2. **Reward the kids who accomplish something special** like saying the memory verse with stickers, stamps, or affirmation. Then reward the others too. Reward for effort or just for being there; leave nobody out. "This is just my way of showing that I love you." Once in a while reward everyone for no particular reason.

3. **Impossible Treat.** Offer something special if the kids can do some impossible feat, like touch the ceiling. Let them try. When it has dawned on them that they cannot earn the treat, and they are feeling sad about that, have an adult step in. He/she might lift each child up to touch the ceiling or else touch it for them. While everyone is enjoying the treat, ask them how they felt and what they thought when nobody could do it. Tell them the activity is like going to heaven. We can't do it; but Jesus can. He will take His children.

4. **Forgive Boo-boos**. Be quick to forgive children who mess up, without making mountains out of anthills. Ask their forgiveness when you react with impatience or in any way let them down.

5. **Promise Keeper**. Make a promise at the beginning of class and then act as if you have forgotten it. Before class ends honor your promise. Talk to the kids about how God is always as good as His word. Following through on promises tells kids they can count on you.

6. **Hide and Seek**. Hide an object for small children to find. Give them hints of where to find it. For older children, have three teams, one of which leaves the room. The other two give clues for finding something. One group always gives true clues. The other sometimes gives true clues. Keep hiding things until the finders catch on that one group is totally dependable. Ask what the activity tells them about God. (He is completely trustworthy.)

their faith, becomes a gentle art that grace impels us to develop. Grace changes the way we view children, the way we speak to them, and the way we treat them. This is what it means to develop a grace-oriented ministry, based on the gospel elements of grace, worship, community, and service.

Developing Inclusive Ministries

Inclusive ministries make it easier for kids to value their church community, getting involved in ministry themselves.

Basically, an inclusive ministry practices Ezekiel 39:28, "I will gather them . . ., not leaving any behind."

Remember the story of the Pied Piper? He led all of the children away, except one—a little boy with a physical handicap. Can you imagine Jesus doing that? He excludes nobody on the basis of race, skin color, language, gender, age, or socio-economic circumstances. In fact, the only people outside the kingdom on the day of judgment are those who chose to be outside.

According to Ezekiel, God wants to save every child. But He takes no person against their will. That's why we do ministry; to encourage every child to make a decision for Jesus. But not every child will accept the ministry of every person. That's why Children's Ministries needs all kinds of people to get involved.

For Children's Ministries to be relational and oriented toward grace, our ministry also needs to become inclusive. We must model the brotherhood of all believers if we value our world church. And we must model unity within the church, if we would fulfill Jesus' ideal for us.

Ways to Practice an Inclusive Ministry

- **Widen your own circle of friendships.** In order for us to develop an inclusive ministry, we must have friends of other cultures and of different generations.
- **Make it "cool"** for youth to reach children for Christ in your church.
- **Use a mix of age levels** and cultures when staffing the various Children's Ministries.
- **Encourage students to make friends of people who are different** from themselves. Encourage them to bring their friends to Children's Ministries events, like Vacation Bible School and Sabbath School.
- **Plan for handicapped children** in your Children's Ministries, even though you may have no handicapped members at present. Pray that God will send people with disabilities to your church. Publicize widely that your church has a ministry for children with handicaps.

- **Begin a Friendship Class** for mentally disabled youth at your church, even if you have only one student for the class. (See chapter 10 for more information.)
- **Choose culturally inclusive pictures**, posters, and felts. Never show a picture of heaven in which everyone is only one race or culture. Think about the negative messages that children get when they see Jesus and the angels continually portrayed as one race.
- **Invite people from other cultures** to visit and tell about their childhood. Or make friends with a children's group in another church. Invite them to a party and try to get to know the children.

Developing Informed Ministries

Jesus words, "Feed my lambs" (John 21:15), are a commission for all His followers. Those who teach children at church are working hand-in-hand with God. Of them, Ellen White says, "It is a noble thing to teach; it is a blessed thing to learn" (Testimonies on Sabbath School Work, p. 17), because every teacher also needs to learn.

The apostle Paul's admonition to Timothy, "Study to show thyself approved unto God, a workman who need not be ashamed" (2 Timothy 2:15), applies to all who teach in the church. Accordingly, to help teachers become more effective and competent in their work for God, the Adventist Church has developed a program of teacher certification for North America.

The most important training for a teacher is personal prayer and Bible study. Ellen White counsels that "managers" of a ministry to children "need to plow deeper." (Testimonies on Sabbath School Work, p. 90). To help teachers dig deeper into the Word, the certification program offers core studies in the Scriptures and specific Children's Ministries training.

What Is Certification? Certification is recognition given upon completion of a series of workshops, seminars, personal study, and practical experience. This study program has been designed to help a person become knowledgeable about the Word of God, the needs of children, and the most effective methods. Those who continue on with the certification process can help to train others. Certification is offered at three levels: teacher, leader, and coordinator.

To begin the program of certification, a participant can write Children's Ministries Certification, Advent*Source*, 5040 Prescott Avenue, Lincoln, NE 68506. Request the Children's Ministries Certification brochure.

Other Educational Opportunities

- **Workshops and conventions**. Conferences and unions offer training events to help teachers and leaders. At these events, experts teach the courses. Sunday School publishers sometimes offer training events that are worthwhile.
- **Satellite and video seminars**. The ACN (Adventist Communications Network) schedule, mailed regularly to the churches, lists all training seminars. Watch for Children's Ministries seminars. Call Advent*Source* in advance of the program to order the participant's workbook. ACN seminar tapes may be purchased from Advent*Source* after the advertised event.
- **Self-study seminars** are available from Advent*Source*. A listing of all available self-study seminar material is available from Advent*Source*. This list is continually being expanded as new materials become available. Check with Advent*Source* annually for a current list.

Professional Ministries Networks

Children's Ministries leaders and teachers need people who can do for each other what people in your everyday network do for you—offer support, enrichment, and help when needed. Everyone who teaches needs this kind of support.

But all too many leaders and teachers feel as if they are all alone in their ministry for children. A network can give such

Conventional Wisdom

10 Laws of Good Networking

1. Believe in yourself enough to ask questions and seek solutions.
2. Respect others and their rights to views and opinions.
3. Be willing to give without demanding or expecting anything in return.
4. Be confident enough to say, "thank you," "I may be wrong," and "I'm sorry" as the need arises.
5. Be friendly; reach out and take an interest in others.
6. Be willing to put in time maintaining the network.
7. Make the most of opportunities when they arise.
8. Don't feel guilty when you need to say "no."
9. Know your goals for ministry and work to achieve them.
10. Work the network all you can for ideas, enrichment, and support.

people a sense of togetherness and the security of knowing that help is only as far away as the telephone or maybe the mailbox. That's why the Adventist Children's Ministries Association is being developed.

The Adventist Children's Ministries Association (ACMA). The ACMA network is for anyone who is involved in the spiritual education of children. The association will provide opportunities to network with others of like interests.

One can use the network to share ideas and information. As they share names and phone numbers, members find out whom they can call to ask questions and solve problems.

ACMA Mission Statement. ACMA serves as a support network for the encouragement and growth of Children's Ministries workers. ACMA seeks to:
- Help churches recognize the importance of ministry to children
- Affirm, encourage, and empower members engaged in this ministry
- Provide opportunities for professional and spiritual growth

- Provide networking opportunities for those engaged in Children's Ministries
- Set standards for certification of Children's Ministries specialists
- Foster unity and facilitate working relationships between all areas of Children's Ministries
- Provide counsel relating to development and review of programs and strategies for Children's Ministries
- Encourage advocacy for children in the church, community, and nation

Membership in ACMA. Membership in ACMA is open to any person involved in the religious education of children. There is an annual membership fee. Benefits include: an annual subscription to Kids' Stuff magazine, ACMA membership card and newsletter, ACMA directory of Children's Ministries, and discounts on ACMA training events. For more information, send your request to ACMA, 5040 Prescott Avenue, Lincoln, NE 68506

Cooperative Ministries

If ministry to children within the congregation is to be effective, all those whose ministry affects children need to work cooperatively, e.g. family life, youth, Pathfinders, Adventurers, Sabbath School, stewardship, health, temperance and pastoral ministries. They will broaden their ministry by cooperating with other Children's Ministries workers. Children will benefit most of all if we all work together instead of in competition with or in isolation from one another.

For many years, literacy advocates have been telling us that if we want to improve the lot of children who are in poverty, we should teach their mothers to read. And it stands to reason, if we would work for the salvation of children, we also need to work with their families. Children's Ministries leaders and teachers need to network with the family life leaders of the church, holding up each other's arms. We need to nurture children with their families.

Try This...

Developing Local Church Initiatives
- Work with the church Family Ministries to teach parents how to use the booklet "*Coming to Jesus, Growing in Him.*" (Advent*Source*)
- Work with the church Stewardship leader to supply children's tithe envelopes (Advent*Source*) and teach the children how to use them.
- Work with the Youth leader to develop an initiative for involving teens in Vacation Bible School, Pathfinders, Adventurers, etc.

Similarly, Children's Ministries supports the Adventurer and Pathfinder programs in the church.

"The nurture we give in Sabbath School can be undone if the children have to turn to secular clubs for socialization, or if the youth department in the church becomes defunct."

—Barbara Manspeaker

Because children are so attracted to youth, whom they hero worship, why not help them find heroes within the church? We need to involve youth in teaching the children of the church. At the same time, many youth can fulfill their need to share Jesus with others.

Children need to see that they are important to the pastor. The children's leader or coordinator can help the pastor see the need for a children's story each week and suggest other ways pastors can boost ministry to children in the church. They can affirm children's leaders and set aside a special Children's Sabbath once a year.

The North American Division has voted Children's Sabbath to be the first Sabbath of October each year. But your church may choose any Sabbath it likes for this purpose.

Resources

ACMA brochure; ACMA Certification brochures, Advent*Source*.
Children's Ministries Catalog. Advent*Source*.
Children's Ministries Department, North American Division.
    Coming to Jesus, Growing in Him. Advent*Source*, 1992.
Children's tithe envelopes. Advent*Source*.
Gillespie, V. Bailey. *The Sounds of Grace in our Churches*.
    Advent*Source*, 1996.
Rice, Gail. *The Textures of Grace in our Schools*. Advent*Source*, 1996.
Tyner, Stuart. *The Colors of Grace in our Homes*. Advent*Source*, 1996.

2 The Ages and Stages of Childhood

Today's Child

Today's child is not like his grandparents were at his age or even like either of his parents were at his age. In fact, children today are not even like the kids of 10 years ago. In *Choices Are Not Child's Play,* Pat Holt says "children today are not inherently so different from children of the past. But society is. The world they live in is very different. And the by-product of that is a very different child."

Think about today's child—the child of the late 1990's. She probably attends day care and may have done so since birth. Because of busy schedules, she is awakened before daylight and hurried to the sitter's. She may not return home until after dark. Much of the day she spends with other children of the same age, learning through structured play.

Today's child spends much time in an electronic bubble. When he is not watching TV or a video, he is likely playing computer games, exploring cyberspace, or talking to friends on the telephone.

Unlike her parents, today's child is multi-cultural. She plays and learns with children of other cultures. She accepts cultural differences as previous generations accepted family differences. Her acceptance of children from other cultures, however, may soon be jeopardized by family attitudes.

Today's child, worldwide, is predominantly urban. We may be kidding ourselves if we picture Adventist children in country settings since 90 percent of us live in cities. As a result, children today are growing up with almost a complete absence of nature. Their parents and teachers are knowledgeable about science, but not intimate with nature.

Children Then and Now

Today's child is growing up on a different planet than we did. But this is the only world a child knows.

How many of the things on the list below were different when you were growing up? Place an X beside each statement that was not typical when you were growing up.

___ Children grow up in different cities from their grandparents, aunts and uncles, and sometimes even from their parents and siblings.

___ Neighborhood streets are full of crime and no longer safe for play.

___ Water, air, and soil pollution threaten personal health and safety.

___ Children see nature on videos or in books, but they don't have hands-on experience in nature or the time to dream about it.

___ Children view world tragedies almost as they happen without setting a foot outside their front door.

___ Children view the private and staged pain of many people without being asked to get involved.

___ Children are bombarded with more and more, bigger and better things and pressured to buy them by every magazine, billboard, and TV commercial.

___ Children are living vicariously; TV culture and the entertainment world live for them more and more.

___ Every family knows somebody whose life has been touched by AIDS.

___ Daily warnings of global warming, loss of the ozone layer, pollution, terrorism, and violence erode a child's sense of security and expectations for the future.

Try This...

Try this activity with your children's ministry leaders and volunteers. Give each person a plain piece of paper and ask them to divide it into thirds. As you fill in each section, discuss the points together. On the first portion, describe the needs of children today. Personalize your list for the children in your congregation.

In the second section, describe how your present programs meet these needs. Use the third section to plan for the future. What needs of today's children do you feel your programs should address?

What might the above mean for Children's Ministries? Check each needs statement below that you think is justified by the facts above.

Children who come to your Children's Ministries programs need...

___ Personal relationships with real people, not more entertainment.

___ Opportunities to encounter the real world: real people, the real out-of-doors, real communities, and real needs.

___ Mentors—people who don't just present a program, but people whom they respect and who show them how to serve.

___ Opportunities to interact so they can see each other as real people.

___ To understand and cooperate with each other, so they can communicate, solve problems, and live in harmony with differences.

___ A chance to accomplish real things.

___ Children need a chance to make real choices and think for themselves.

___ Trusted adults who hear what children say about their fears and dreams.

___ A safe environment. Not just safe physically, but safe emotionally (where they are accepted for themselves) and socially (where all differences are accepted, acknowledged, and valued).

Basic Needs of Children

All children have certain basic needs as well as needs that are specific to their age and stage of development.

> The basic needs of children are for . . .
>
> *Physical*
> - Food
> - Warmth
> - Shelter
>
> *Mental*
> - Power—to make choices and follow plans
>
> *Emotional*
> - A sense of belonging
> - Approval and recognition
> - Expressions of unconditional love and acceptance
> - Freedom within defined boundaries
> - Humor—a chance to laugh
>
> *Spiritual*
> - An all-knowing, loving, caring God
> - Forgiveness of wrongs and a chance to start over
> - Assurance of acceptance with God
> - Experience in prayer, answers to prayer
> - A chance to grow in grace and in the knowledge of God

The Beginner Child

In the Seventh-day Adventist Church, the beginner (cradle roll) division has in the past been for children age birth through two years.

The new curriculum for beginners targets children ages birth through two years. However, both the beginner and the kindergarten materials are adaptable to 3-year-olds.

In order to understand beginner children, ages birth through two years, it is helpful to note characteristics of their growth and development.

Rule of Thumb: Seat children so their feet easily touch the ground. For children under 18 months use walkers (without wheels).

Physical
- Vary greatly in their physical development
- Are growing rapidly
- Tire easily
- Cannot sit still for long

Mental
- Have an attention span of only one or two minutes
- Learn by active involvement and imitation rather than by instruction
- Learn best one mini-step at a time
- Focus attention on what they see and/or touch

Emotional
- Are extremely egocentric — centered in themselves
- Fear separation from parents
- Cry easily; one crying child sets other children crying
- Express their needs by crying. The crying usually stops when the child's needs are met
- Become attached to adults who show love and acceptance of them

Spiritual
- Senses attitudes of respect, joy, and anticipation in connection with church, the Bible, and Jesus
- Can identify pictures of Jesus and lisp His name
- Will fold hands (briefly) for the blessing before meals and kneel (again briefly) for prayer

Developmental Needs

In addition to the basic needs listed on page 24, two-year-olds need to experience:
- Power—to have a chance to manipulate objects, events, people
- Freedom—to make choices, to interact in learning situations, to sometimes move about at will
- Independence—to do some things unaided
- Security—to feel safe

The Kindergarten Child

In the Seventh-day Adventist Church, the kindergarten division traditionally has included children ages 4-6. Today, we advocate kindergarten for children ages 3-5, because children of that age range usually attend day care together.

The description below is true of children ages 3-5.

Physical
- Start developing large muscle coordination
- Lack a sure sense of balance
- Are extremely active
- Tire easily; but soon revive after resting
- Lack fine muscle coordination
- Are curious and like to explore their environment
- Learn by exploring

Mental
- Are capable of limited listening and understanding without the help of a visual cue, such as seeing the object being discussed
- Have a quick memory
- Memorize things they don't understand

A child's attention span, in minutes, is their age plus one. An average 3-year-old has a potential attention span of four minutes, provided they are interested in what is happening.

- Enjoy repetition—provided they don't tire
- Are beginning to reason from simple cause to effect
- Make some generalizations—often incorrectly
- Learn best by active participation
- Have a short attention span—3-6 minutes

Emotional
- Cry easily
- Are capable of verbalizing emotional responses
- Learn to delay gratification of needs without losing equilibrium
- Experience the full spectrum of negative emotions
- Learn ways to express negative emotions

Social/Relational
- Are self-centered—the world revolves around them
- Play alone in the presence of their friends, rather than playing with their friends
- Like to make friends and be with friends

Developmental Needs
In addition to the basic needs listed on page 24, kindergarten children need:
- Freedom—to choose and to explore within limits
- Power—to have some autonomy in learning situations
- Limits—safe boundaries that are set by parents and teachers
- Fun—learning through play; enjoying success
- Discipline and training—to provide safety and structure in their lives

Spiritual Needs
Kindergarten children need to know:
- God loves and cares for them
- How to show respect for God
- How to respect themselves; this comes from knowing that God made them, knows them, and values them
- The difference between right and wrong
- How to choose the right with God's help

The Primary Child

In the Seventh-day Adventist Church, the primary division has traditionally been for children of grades 2-4. Today we recommend including first graders in primary. Large churches may have two primary divisions:

Primary I - grades 1, 2 (ages 6-7)
Primary II - grades 3, 4 (ages 8-9)

The following characteristics are typical of primary-age children.

Physical
- Show good muscle coordination and balance
- Behave in a boisterous and energetic manner
- Learn eye-hand coordination for fine-muscle skills
- Willingly practice so as to learn new skills
- Are somewhat far-sighted until 8-years old
- Are good singers

Mental
- Like to demonstrate their newly-acquired reading skills; however, many through age 9 need help finding and reading Bible texts
- Are literal thinkers; need objects and pictures to help them understand
- Are learning to distinguish between fact and fancy
- Are curious and observant, asking lots of questions
- Learn best from hands-on experience with concrete objects
- Are capable of prolonged interest and concentration
- Apply simple, logical thought to practical situations
- Memorize easily
- Show an interest in the faraway and long ago
- Have limited understanding of time and historical sequence

Children who begin school late or are homeschooled should be promoted with their age or grade level, at the end of the school year. Children should not be held back.

- Are strongly committed to fairness; want those who break the rules to be punished
- Enjoy discussing experiences and new ideas
- Are fond of stories
- Like using new words

Emotional
- Appreciate variety within a fairly stable routine; a complete change of program can upset younger primaries.
- Are learning to control negative emotions, expressing them in socially acceptable ways
- Need adults to model self-control
- Fear death and divorce
- Are motivated by recognition

Social/Relational
- Enjoy group games, projects, quizzes, and activities
- Are naturally boisterous and energetic
- Like adults and seek relationships with them; want to please them
- Want to make friends, especially best friends, with their peers
- Can be "little legalists", wanting to know the rules and to apply them to other people
- Want to belong to clubs and groups; family and church are important to them

Spiritual
- Understand some simple religious symbolism
- Have an interest in God
- Willingly believe what the church teaches
- Want to be told what to believe
- Understand enough about sin and salvation to choose Jesus as Savior and best Friend
- Want to please God
- Make prayer a part of daily life if encouraged to do so
- Willingly accept their responsibility as stewards if given the opportunity
- Imitate models of Christian living

Developmental Needs

In addition to their basic needs, primary children have a need to:
- Develop a sense of responsibility
- Develop a sense of accomplishment
- Grow in self-esteem
- Learn social and academic skills
- Balance personal freedom with parental limits

Spiritual Needs

Primary children need:
- To know God loves and cares for them
- To develop a personal relationship with Jesus, and see Him as their Friend
- Ready access to God through prayer
- To experience forgiveness and mercy
- Assurance of acceptance with God—without it, they experience fear and guilt
- To know the law of God; they will apply it as a standard of living
- Help to offer mercy and forgiveness to those who wrong them

The Junior Student

In the Adventist Church, juniors are students in grades 5-6 (ages 10, 11). Earliteens, students in grades 7-8 (ages 12, 13), often share the Sabbath School program with juniors. Earliteens, however, are at a different stage of development with their own specific needs.

Note some characteristics of a junior child's growth and development. Juniors typically:

Physical
- Mature at different rates; some girls may experience the growth spurt that signals adolescence
- Are energetic, loud, talkative, and imaginative
- Have well-developed verbal skills

Mental
- Are on the brink of doing abstract thinking
- Like to figure cause and effect
- Have a rapidly-increasing attention span
- Discover ways to answer their own questions
- Need to have abstract words and concepts explained to them
- Begin to question authority
- Are capable of thinking and reasoning

Emotional
- Lack self-esteem
- Are subject to mood swings
- Get bored unless they see the purpose in what they are doing
- Crave success and affirmation
- Are acquiring values
- Take themselves seriously

Rule of Thumb — Do not call juniors or earliteens students "children." They refer to each other as "kids" and do not mind being referred to as kids, people, team, troops or gang.

Social/Relational
- Care about pleasing their peers
- Are hero-worshipers
- Are action-oriented
- Start to develop gender roles

Spiritual
- Want Bible teaching to be practical, related to their life
- Are ready to make salvation decisions
- Are developing their consciences
- Feel responsibility for their sins
- Are rule-oriented
- Are looking for adult models

Developmental Needs

Juniors have the basic needs of childhood plus the need to:
- Be responsible
- Achieve competence
- Grow in self-esteem
- Master social, academic, and physical skills
- Earn from parents a greater measure of personal freedom

Spiritual Needs

Juniors need:
- To know God loves and understands them
- A Savior who can give them victory over sin
- Confirmation that God answers prayer and encouragement to trust Him
- To know what God has done for others and what they personally can expect from Him
- To know how God affects their daily lives
- To experience forgiveness and freedom from guilt

Try This...

Tape together sheets from a flip chart or from an end roll of newsprint. Ask a child of the age level that you teach to lie on the paper while you draw around him/her. See how much information you can find out about children of this age, by questioning the child or the children in your class. Record your findings within the outline on the paper. Compare what you found from the child/children to the characteristics noted in this chapter. Are there any similarities? Any differences?

The Earliteen Student

In the Adventist Church, earliteens are students in grades 7-8 (ages 12, 13). Earliteens are preadolescent; they can behave like adolescents one minute and children, the next. And because kids reach puberty at varying ages, it is difficult to list characteristics that will be true for all. Some earliteen students will look and behave much of the time like juniors; others look and behave more like adolescants. Within this wide range of development, however, certain characteristics hold fairly true.

Physical
- Mature at widely different rates; girls generally experiencing a growth spurts before boys of the same chronological age
- (Most of them) reach puberty during the earliteen years
- Want action and want it now
- Can be quite awkward as they cope with growth spurts
- Often look more grown up than they act

Mental
- Think in the abstract quite well, but still need examples, synonyms, or word pictures to illustrate new concepts
- Understand symbolism once it has been explained
- Capable of engaging in discussion and debate
- Have long attention span—provided they are interested in the topic
- Test the boundaries of convention and knowledge
- Interested in making money (boys more so than girls)
- Beginning to question everything look for authoritative answers
- Reject illogical reasoning or rules

Emotional
- Lack self-confidence and self-esteem
- Experience wild mood swings
- Get bored easily
- Be always testing the values they grew up with
- Take themselves seriously
- Appreciate adults who are low-keyed and who joke with them
  Social/Relational
- Cave in to peer pressure; often afraid to take a stand
- Be somewhat clumsy in relating to each other
- Avoid doing anything in isolation from the group
- Extremely interested in the opposite sex

- Fear being singled out as different
- Seek close friendships within a tight group

Spiritual
- Question spiritual truths that they previously had accepted
- Challenge religious beliefs while at the same time needing help to clarify them
- Need to make a recommitment to God
- Need constant reminders of God's love and grace
- Need to hear adults talk about their personal faith
- Want a practical religion to live by

Developmental Needs

Earliteens have the basic needs of childhood, as described on p. 24, plus the need to
- Collect and sift through information
- Make more of their own decisions
- Express their individuality in various ways (usually with varying degrees of success)
- Crave affirmation
- Need increased freedoms from parental control and corresponding increases in their responsibilities
- Need more time with peers
- Need increased emotional distance from parents
- Need authoratative standards by which to judge right from wrong

Spiritual Needs

Earliteens need:
- To know that there is a God
- To be told again and again that there is nothing they can do to make God love them more or anything they can do to make Him love them less
- A Savior who can give them victory over sin
- To learn how to forgive and to accept forgiveness
- To experience forgiveness and freedom from guilt

- To be told what is in it for them if they commit to living God's way
- What God has done for others and will do for them
- To admit that they need a Savior

The Developmental Task for Earliteens

Earliteens are beginning to struggle with the task of discovering their inner, personal identity and making decisions based on their own identity instead of their group's identity. They will continue to struggle with their identity through the high school years.

Resources

Betz, Charles H. *How to Teach the Bible with Power.* Review and Herald, 1995.

Constance, Kamii and Janet Ewing. "Basing Teaching on Piaget's Constructivism." *Childhood Education Annual Theme Issue* 1996, pages 260-262.

Habenicht, Donna and Anne Bell. *How to Teach Children in Sabbath School.* Review and Herald, 1983.

Habenicht, Donna. *How to Help Your Child Really Love Jesus.* Review and Herald, 1994.

Holt, Pat and Grace Ketterman. *Choices Are Not Child's Play.* Harold Shaw Publishers, 1990.

Louv, Richard. *Childhood's Future.* Anchor Books, 1990.

3 Leading a Child to Jesus

> "*If properly instructed, very young children may have correct views of their state as sinners and of the way of salvation through Christ.*"
> —Ellen G. White, *Counsels on Sabbath School Work,* pages 79-80.

The whole point of our ministry to children is that we want to help them commit their lives to God. Knowing the difference that commitment makes in a person can help us shape the kind of spiritual education that we offer. We also need to remember the five imperatives of commitment.

Five Imperatives for Committed Children and Youth

- **Goal-oriented spiritual education.** Teach kids at church what they need in order to remain committed. The eight points of commitment (see page 38) can be part of our mission as teachers in the church.
- **Supportive family life.** Spiritual education at church has a better chance of taking root when the soil of the spirit and the mind has been worked by family worship and lesson study in the home. Ellen White admonishes, "Parents should take special interest in the religious education of their children that they may have a more thorough knowledge of the Scriptures." She

suggests that parents spend more time on the Sabbath School lesson study with the child and less time on their outward appearance.

- **Warm, caring church community.** The folks at church have more of an impact on the commitment of kids today than members realize. Kids particularly need the church to be a place where they can ask questions and find answers. They need to be allowed to help at church and to feel accepted and needed.
- **Christian social settings.** Kids need to find their friends and their social life among church members. Adventist schools and academies provide a social setting for kids, as do summer youth camps, Pathfinders, and camporees. Combining the social with the religious helps kids integrate faith and lifestyle.
- **Christian school.** Kids who attend Adventist schools and have committed teachers have an advantage in learning commitment.

Try This...

Purchase a copy of the colorful booklet *"Coming to Jesus, Growing in Him"* (Advent*Source*) for each child in your class. Read the steps to Jesus and give a booklet to each child. Older children can read the book and explain the points to a friend in class.

The first part of the booklet leads the children into a commitment and gives the assurance of salvation. The last half of the booklet explains how to grow in Jesus.

Leading a Child to Jesus

Ellen White, in *Counsels on Sabbath School Work*, admonishes workers: "Never rest till every child in your class is brought to the saving knowledge of Christ." How does one bring a child "to the saving knowledge of Christ?"

When leading a child step-by-step to a commitment of their life to Jesus, what does one say? And what do kids need to know? The following steps have been found meaningful to many in helping kids process what they know, feel, and experience of God.

Conventional Wisdom

Pointers of Leading Kids to Jesus

As you begin leading your students through *A Child's Steps to Jesus*, keep in mind these important points.

- Give kids an opportunity to commit themselves to Jesus without pressuring them.
- The real commitment to Jesus is not done as a group, but individually.
- Children can tell in their own words that they want to belong to Jesus.
- Don't assume kids understand they have made a commitment to Jesus.
- Children don't always understand abstract ideas like a commitment to Jesus; so ask children to share what they believe about Jesus saving them.
- Avoid telling kids they have made a commitment; they alone know if they have.
- If a child is not sure whether or not he or she has received Jesus, the child probably has not. Receiving Jesus is not a once-in-a-lifetime event; Christians need to renew their commitment often.
- You and the child need to talk to the child's parents about the child's commitment. This can be an opportunity to present the gospel to non-Christian parents.

1. Begin with love.

Jesus loves us all the time, no matter what we do. Nothing can make Jesus love us more or less than He does right now. (John 3:16; 1 John 4:8; Steps to Christ, chapter 1)

2. Show their need.

Doing wrong is called sin. Everyone has sinned. No person is good enough by themselves to be in heaven. (Romans 3:23; Revelation 21:27; John 8:21,24; Steps to Christ, pages 9-10)

3. Show the way.

Jesus, the sinless Son of God, died for our sin. He is the only way to heaven. (John 3:16; I Corinthians 15:3-4; Steps to Christ, pages 13-15)

Stop after each step and ask the child how he feels about what you read together. Do not press the child to receive Jesus.

—Noelene Johnsson

Try This...

Take somebody—a child, friend, or spouse—through the steps to Jesus. They might say, "I need to try out something I learned. Would you let me explain it to you?"

Characteristics of Committed Children and Youth

The following eight characteristics can be seen as evidence of a mature commitment to faith. Our ministry to children at church should foster development in these areas. In this sense, the following can also be goals for Children's Ministries. Committed children and youth are like this; they

1. **Know a personal Christ.** They need to know that God loves them and cares about them personally.

2. **Understand grace.** God loves them beyond anything they deserve. He is on their side. Their salvation is not based on what they do; they could never be good enough. But Jesus is; He died in their place. All they have to do is to believe and accept it.

3. **Learn Scripture.** Scripture needs to be part of their daily time with God. Scripture stored in the memory can save lives—provided they understand and think about what they are learning.

4. **Be morally responsible.** It isn't enough to know what is right and wrong. Children need to value rightness—be committed to doing what is right and living God's way.

5. **Accept the community of all believers.** A commitment to God and an understanding of grace should make a difference in the way we relate to other people, including those who are different from us.

6. **Share Christ.** In response to God's grace, they need to share His love with others, by telling what God has done for them. This witness can be through lifestyle as well as a spoken message.

7. **Get involved in service.** They show their love for God by serving the least of His children on earth.

8. **Enjoy high self-regard.** A person who grows in faith, "in favor with God and men," cannot help but feel confident and self-assured.

4. Help them receive Jesus.

We pray, admitting our need, asking forgiveness for sin, accepting Jesus as the way, and asking Him to make us new. (John 1:12; Revelation 3:20; Steps to Christ, pages 30-31)

5. Give them assurance.

When we receive Jesus, we are His child and have a place in His kingdom and in heaven. (John 3:36; Hebrews 13:5; Steps to Christ pages 32-33)

Helping Children Grow in Jesus

Children also need to know how to keep their conversion experience—how to grow in Jesus. The following pointers are helpful.

- **Teach them to pray daily.**

We can talk to God every day! Talking with God is called prayer. We can thank Him and tell Him things that make us happy or sad—He's always listening. (Psalm 92:1-2; Psalm 32:6)

- **Teach them what to do about guilt.**

Guilt is the feeling you have when you sometimes do wrong and feel bad inside. God still loves you. He takes away those feelings when we ask Him to forgive our sins. (Isaiah 1:18; 1 John 1:9)

- **Teach them to grow through Bible study.**

Reading God's Word, the Bible, helps you to know what God wants you to do. He wants you to grow happier, more obedient and more helpful. (2 Timothy 3:15; Psalm 119: 11)

- **Teach dependence on Jesus.**

Trying to make good choices on our own doesn't work! But we can make good choices with God's help. Every day we can ask Him to show us the best way to live. (John 14:15; Exodus 20:1-12)

- **Help them serve.**

Telling others how happy we are to know God is called witnessing. You and I witness about Jesus' love in what we say and do. God wants us to tell others! (Acts 1:8)

Great Idea! Try This...

For each of the eight goals of spiritual education suggest one activity that kids in your class or family could do. Tell how the activity might help the child toward that goal.

For instance, to help children know a personal Christ, try "Asking God's Empty Chair." Set an empty chair beside you and say, "Imagine Jesus sitting here." Each child in turn tells what they would ask Jesus if He were there. Explain that Jesus is there and hears them. He wants to help them find the answer through Bible study, prayer, and knowledgeable adults. They will know when they have found their answer. You can adapt this activity to surface problems they would like Jesus to solve.

Resources

Case, Steve. *It's My Choice - Junior Baptismal Guide.* Review & Herald, 1996.

Children's Ministries Department, North American Division. *Coming to Jesus, Growing in Him.* AdventSource, 1992.

Cornforth, Fred and Kelly Blue. *Creative Bible Learning Activities - 101 Ideas for Junior Teen Leaders.* AdventSource, 1995.

Habenicht, Donna. *How to Help Your Child Really Love Jesus.* Review & Herald, 1994.

Habenicht, Donna and Anne Bell. *How to Teach Children in Sabbath School.* Review & Herald, 1983.

White, Ellen G. *Counsels on Sabbath School Work..* Review & Herald, 1938.

4 Faith Development and the Life Stages

Luke's simple statement, "And Jesus grew in wisdom and stature," (Luke 2:52, NIV) sums up Jesus' development through the ages and stages of childhood. Even more important, the statement clearly recognizes wisdom (mental) and stature (physical) as separate areas of development. But Luke adds, "and in favor with God and man," suggesting spiritual and social growth or faith development.

Defining Faith

What is faith? Check the following statements about faith that agree with your experience to this point.

__ 1. "Now faith is being sure of what we hope for and certain of what we do not see." (Hebrews 11:1, NIV)
__ 2. "Jesus (is) the author and perfector of our faith." (Hebrews 12:2)
__ 3. "Faith without deeds is dead" (James 2:26) and "cannot save" (2:14).
__ 4. "Faith comes by hearing the message, and the message is heard through the word of Christ." (Romans 10:17)
__ 5. "Continues to grow…" (2 Cor 10:15)
__ 6. Faith, when tested, "develops perseverance." (James 1:3)
__ 7. Faith is the means by which "Jesus Christ will continue to live in your hearts." (Ephesians 3:17)

Faith is all of the above and more. As one chooses Jesus a bond of trust is forged. This relationship is daily strengthened through prayer, Bible study, and a multitude of choices. Faith grows and expands with development until it is able to withstand severe stress and testing.

Faith is a living, growing relationship with God that develops and grows throughout one's life.

Modeling Unconditional Love

Model unconditional love for children at home or in church by trying some of the following ideas.

- Offer a prize for the child who completes a task. Accept their efforts. Reward every child—even the one who tries least.
- Have a party for no reason at all except to show love.
- Rubber stamp a child's hand every time she does something praiseworthy. Then stamp the hand for no special reason except to say, "I'm glad you are trying."
- Offer to light a candle for every year of a child's age. Then light lots more because you value the child more than just for years.
- Promise a story by candlelight "tomorrow" or "next week" if the children learn the memory verse (or whatever). Then gather them together and light the candle right away. Tell them a story of grace and explain that you loved them so much you couldn't wait until tomorrow. Then ask the kids if they want to show their love by completing the task you suggested earlier.

John H. Westerhoff III likens faith to a tree trunk. The young trunk has few rings; older trunks have many. The rings of faith growth occur as a result of life experiences and in interacting with others and with God. Westerhoff identifies four main stages of faith development.

1. Experienced Faith

- **The Key** to experienced faith in early childhood is observation and reaction. Children observe love and faith in their interaction with adults and react to what they experience. At this stage they are too young to consciously think about faith, but nevertheless, demonstrate unwavering faith.

- **The Needs** at this stage are to experience trust, love, and acceptance. Little children need a few trusted and loving adults in their lives. Sometimes pets provide the love and acceptance adults are too busy to give.
- **Foster Faith** at this stage through warmth, hugs, active listening, and countless experiences of unconditional love.

2. Belonging Faith

- **The Key** to faith for a primary-age child is a sense of belonging. Children of this age have a keen sense of the order of things. They are also great "joiners." They want to belong to a church that is bigger than their family and to clubs within the church.
- **The Needs** for children at this stage of faith development are:
  - A sense of authority. They are satisfied to have their "why" questions answered, "because the Bible" or "because the Adventist Church" says so.
  - To hear the story of the community they belong to. Stories of God's working in Bible times and in the beginnings of their church feed the child's growing faith.
  - Experiences of awe and wonder, which are partly what worship is about.
  - To sense they are wanted at church, they are accepted by their teachers and peers, and they are missed when absent.
- **Foster Faith** by filling the above needs through stories, drama, art, and creative worship experiences in a warm, accepting atmosphere.

Ways to Foster Belonging

- Help children learn the faith stories of their congregation or extended family. Have them ask people, "Why are you a Seventh-day Adventist?" and report the stories and responses they hear.
- To give kids a sense of church family, help children make a photo album of people in the congregation, including children and babies. Talk about how church members are a family. How is church like a club? How is it different?

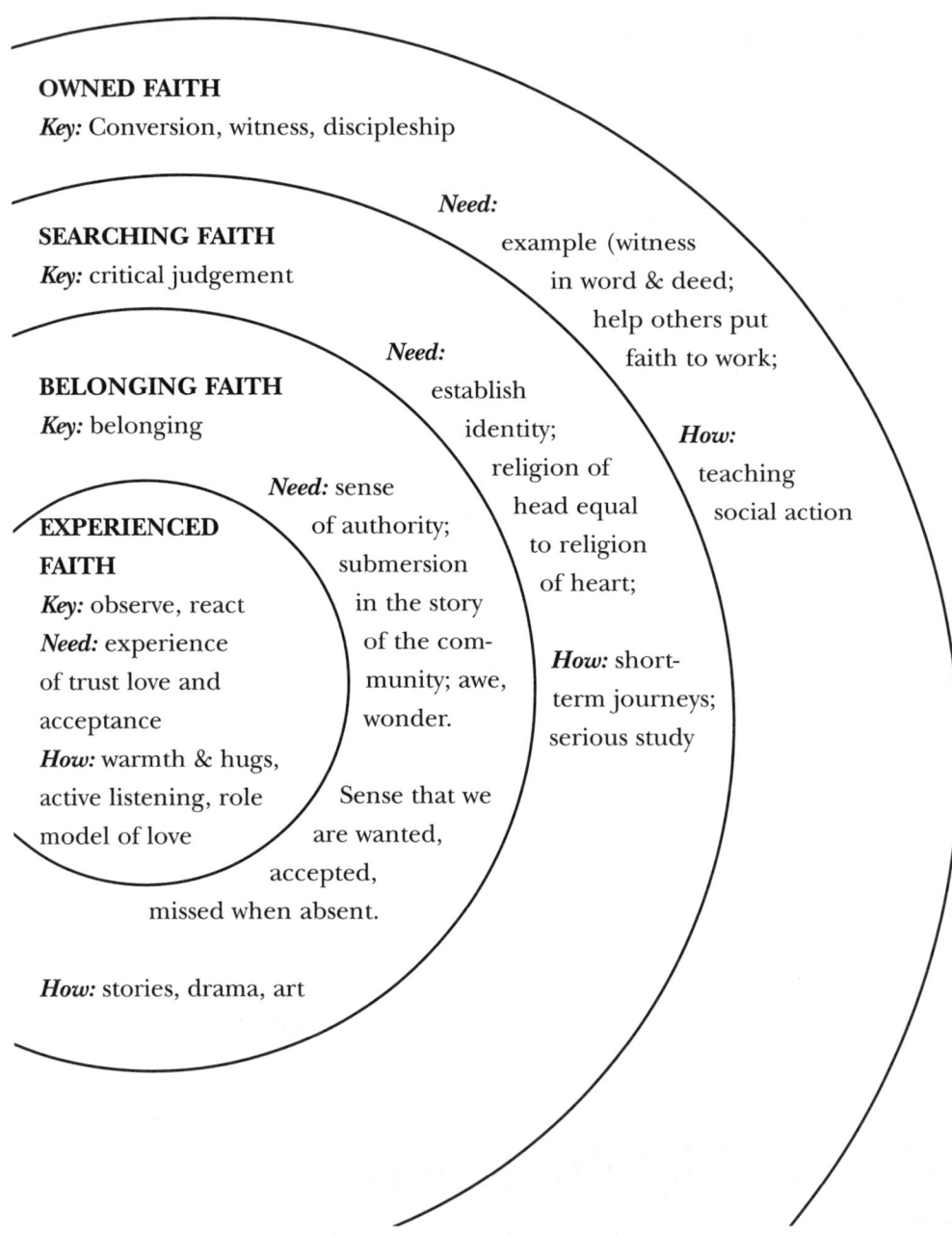

This chart was created by John H. Westerhoff III, one of several theorists concerned with faith development. Their theories offer us a useful guide to understanding how we grow in the faith.

3. Searching Faith

- **The Key** element of the adolescent's searching faith is critical judgment. For the pre-adolescent, quoting authorities is not enough. They want to examine all the information for themselves.
- **The Needs** at this stage of faith development are:
  - To establish their own identity. They are questioning and examining their beliefs, their lifestyle, their appearance, all authority, and anything they identify with, in an effort to define themselves.
  - To know that the religion of the head is equal to the religion of the heart. This compels kids to ask searching questions that challenge the adult's beliefs. They become critical of any explanations that cannot be supported by logic, good sense, and scientific inquiry. Adults need to accept the questions without feeling threatened, working with the kids to find the answers.
  - To be needed in the faith community.
- **Foster Faith** in adolescents through serious Bible study, short-term journeys, mission trips and service opportunities.

Encouraging a Searching Faith

Pack the earliteen group into a van and go visit in quick succession a hospital nursery, a child care center, a court of law, a nursing home and the city morgue. Plan ahead so that your visit will be expected. Ask for a short tour and introduction at each facility. Space the visits to take the entire day.

Make the connection: Read together Jeremiah 1:5 after visiting the nursery; Jeremiah 1:6, 7 after the child care center; Proverbs 14:12 and Isaiah 48:17, 18 after the court; Ecclesiastes 3:1-8 at the nursing home; and Psalm 23 on the way home. Allow time for kids to talk about what they see. Don't labor any point or try to preach to them. Instead, ask them how they felt about the journey.

4. Owned Faith

- **The Keys** to a lasting faith for the adult are: conversion, witnessing, and discipleship. While conversion in pre-adolescence or childhood was real, the individual experiences it again in terms of a faith that they have taken responsibility for and ownership of.
- **The Needs** in adulthood are to be an example, to find opportunities to witness by word and by lifestyle, and to help others put faith to work.
- **Foster Faith** through teaching opportunities and social action as well as by personal Bible study and prayer.

How Children Think

Let's take a look at how children think at various stages and relate those patterns to their spiritual experience. Four stages of thinking, from birth through teen years, are briefly described with suggestions on how to instruct learners at each stage.

The model is borrowed from Swiss developmental psychologist, Jean Piaget, who helped us understand how people think at various stages of cognitive development.

"Labeling individuals for their stage of development is not helpful. Neither should one view one stage of faith development as being better or worse than another."

—Barbara Manspeaker

Stage I—Birth to two years

For the first two years of life a child's ability to understand is based on exploration of the world through the senses. The child learns about objects by placing them into the mouth, banging things together or dropping them on the floor.

The child watches an object being moved about the room and notices if the object remains the same or is changed. Sitting up, crawling, walking, climbing and running are also means of discovery. A Stage I thinker processes only what the senses focus on.

When teaching Stage I Learners...

- Plan physical activities like walking to God's house or having a classroom "nature" walk.
- Give children objects to touch. The objects should be large enough that they cannot be swallowed.
- Vary activities by alternating action with quiet or listening activities.
- Provide a variety of materials and textures for the child to handle.
- Use familiar materials to attract their attention—relate the object or experience to spiritual concepts, such as: God's love, creation, or their praise and thanksgiving.
- Keep calm in every situation. Speak quietly; avoid hurry. Proceed at a child's pace.
- Model for them how to express their feelings to God. Show a variety of flowers, then pray, "Jesus, we thank you for the flowers." They may try to repeat it with you!
- Give clear impressions by repeating stories in exact words. Use visuals and activities to focus their attention on the story.
- Speak of Jesus as a friend. Help the child feel confident of His love.

Count Down

Encourage parents to teach the concept of a Seventh-day Sabbath by telling little children every morning, "Today is (Monday). There are (five) more days to Sabbath."

Stage II—Ages two to seven

From the ages of two to seven, a child's thinking can operate independently from the body's senses. During this time, a child's imagination seems to know no boundaries—simple objects like a pencil or a block of wood can be transformed instantly into a plane, dog, banana or a shooting star!

Not surprisingly, the child's thinking is quite inaccurate. Space relationships aren't fully understood — tall is big and large is valuable. If asked to choose between a nickel and a dime, the Stage II child will pick up a nickel "because it's bigger" and therefore more valuable.

Gullibility also characterizes a child in Stage II. Santa Claus is a real person and so is the tooth fairy. Talking animals, though unrealistic, fit the ways that children naturally think at this stage. Stage II thinkers find the Bible story of Balaam's donkey and the great fish that swallowed Jonah to be completely appropriate ways for God to communicate. Miracles are entirely credible to these young minds.

No problem is too big for their God to handle—they pray in absolute confidence. This characteristic of children is surely what Jesus referred to in Matthew 18:3, "Except you become as little children, you will by no means enter the kingdom of heaven."

A Stage II thinker accepts God as a real person and accepts and returns His love. Children at this age want to please God and can choose Jesus as their friend. But they are also very literal. This is illustrated by the little boy who said, when the doctor asked to listen to the boy's heart, "I don't have a heart. I gave it to Jesus."

When Teaching Stage II Learners...
- Plan varied activities by mixing action activities with quiet, "processing" times.
- Teach through dramatic play—they learn by doing!
- Emphasize Bible truths of sharing and helping. Show how they can please Jesus through their acts of kindness. Adopt a class service project (for older members).
- Teach them to express joy and praise to God through music.
- Give them opportunities to think! Present a problem and let them solve it on their level of understanding. Give them time to reason out an answer and then explain their solution.
- Present the lesson so the students can place themselves "in" the story—relate the lesson to their daily life.

Stage III—Ages seven to eleven

From approximately the age of seven to the age of eleven (or even later) a child's thinking ability centers on what is concrete and tangible. What is real is what is experienced.

As relieved as adults might be that the child has become more realistic, the realism comes with a certain loss. If what is real is what is experienced, then is God real?

These Stage III children seek first-hand confirmation of what they learn. When the pastor shares that Jesus is in heaven interceding on our behalf, these children ask: "If Jesus is in heaven, how can He simultaneously help the person who is homeless or in prison?

Although some childish perspectives drop away, these years are a fertile time for information storage. This is the age when memorization is quick and facts are easily remembered. Bible quizzes, Bible sword drills and other Scripture contests are popular.

"Loving" God must be spelled out in concrete terms for these students. That's why simple service projects are so enthusiastically supported. The Ten Commandments can be appreciated because they are so straightforward; but the Sermon on the Mount, with all its multiple applications, is a bit confusing.

"Stage III thinkers are not only literalists: they tend to be little legalists. Preoccupied with questions of right and wrong, they want behavior spelled out in rules—which they galdly apply to others."

—Noelene Johnsson

Symbols are not well understood at this stage. When you share passionately what the cross means to you, a Stage III student is

Bible Story Role Play

Use "Bible Drama T-shirts" to dress kids for their roles. These are oversize t-shirts with pre-printed designs depicting Jesus, an angel, a shepherd, a woman, a king, and a queen. These are great for encouraging kids to re-tell Bible stories in their own style!

For instance: To tell the story of Queen Esther, make a cardboard "castle entrance" to your classroom. Tell the children to watch out for the moat! Dress child volunteers in appropriate Bible T-shirts (King, Queen, Woman). Provide small treats such as grapes and wheat crackers for the "banquet." Hand out instruments for the court musicians and don't forget to spray a little floral perfume for that royal atmosphere! (available from Advent*Source*)

amazed that anyone can get so emotional about two pieces of wood! And the Communion service is tasteless wheat crackers with only a swallow of grape juice!

Their most difficult questions have to do with whether or not we will need wings to fly in heaven, or if our pets will be there.

When Teaching Stage III Learners...

- Show how they can use their energy for the Lord! Organize a class service project.
- Make handwork purposeful—with practical use and a connection to the lesson.
- Provide variety in your lesson presentation and surprise them by occasionally changing the order of your class routine.
- Use drama, role plays, and readings that pose a situation or problem for them to solve.
- Help them feel secure in God's love. Affirm their special gifts.
- Explain the "why" of rules.
- Boys this age admire strength and power. Show them how God enabled men and women in the Bible to be strong to do His will. Encourage Bible reading as a "faith-strengthening" exercise.
- Present short biographies of godly heroes for them to imitate.

Stage IV—Age eleven through the teen years

Stage IV thinking comes gradually. It may begin as early as 11 years of age, but for most it occurs during the teen years.

Talk Sheets

Create your own Sabbath School "Earliteen Talk Sheets!" A Talk Sheet is a reproducible handout on the latest earliteen topics—parents, divorce, heaven, racism, friends, worry, happiness, etc. Make a master sheet and include:

- teen topic
- pertinent Scripture references
- open-ended questions (that don't require a "yes" or "no" answer)
- neat graphics

Physiologically, the left and right half of the brain fuse together. The person is finally able to think about thinking! Logic and abstract thought become possible and symbols can be understood rather than just memorized.

How can you tell when a person is moving into Stage IV thinking? They start asking questions! Everything is "Why?" Rather than preventing, ignoring, or disdaining this question, it's best to encourage their questions so issues can be discussed within the home, school or church. This is the age for using Talk Sheets and discussion starters in a small group setting.

When Teaching Stage IV Learners...

- Listen when they talk.
- Remember your own teen experiences and relate them when relevant.
- Keep a sense of humor.
- Don't overreact. Teens love to share controversial ideas just to see your reaction!
- Truly care about them. Arrange group activities outside of the classroom situation.
- Avoid using abstract Christian jargon.
- Keep the program active and varied to keep their interest.
- Use Bible Learning Activities (see Chapter 7), interactive video, Talk Sheets, etc.

Buried Alive!

Ahead of time, bring to junior class stacks of newspapers, garbage bags, and a blanket.

Divide the class into groups of 4-6. One person from each group lies on the floor (or blanket) with arms outstretched. The others gather around and toss newspapers on the person until they are completely covered. Halt the activity when the bodies are sufficiently buried. (Make sure they can still breathe!)

The "buried" person stays under the newspapers while classmates discuss the kinds of things kids can feel buried under (parent's expectations, school pressure, work, guilt, sin). Kids now break out from their cover. How does it feel to be free of all the clutter? Read Luke 16:13.

Try This...

Scan this chart for an overview of the eight life stages, their tasks and resulting virtue.

The Life Stages	How Achieved
Infants through First Year	Trust is learned when their physical and emotional needs are anticipated and met.*
Second Year	Autonomy is learned as they begin doing things for themselves.
Third through Fifth Years	They gain self-confidence as they take initiative to follow through on tasks.
Sixth Year through Puberty	Completing job assignments, learning recognition for both effort and results.
Adolescence	Learning one's place in family, school and church. Discovering one's gifts and talents.
Young Adult	Learning the value of shared love and commitment.
Middle Age	Taking part in service work; share expertise with others.
Old Age	By passing on virtues, accepting changes that can and cannot be made; accepting death.

Swiss educational psychologist, Jean Piaget, suggested eight stages in a person's life. He named the stages according to the chief developmental task of each stage. The favorable outcome of mastering the task is a virtue—a positive character trait. A person who masters each stage of development is systematically developing character. So perhaps Luke's "in favor with God and man" suggests character development. Notice that faith—as in trust—is foundational to character development. Psychologists tell us that mastery of each successive virtue is dependent upon mastery of the previous tasks.

Developmental Task	Resulting Virtue
To learn trust	Hope
To become autonomous	Right use of the will
To develop initiative	Self-confidence
To become industrious	Competence
To identify one's role	Loyalty
To learn intimacy	Love
To be productive for the good of self and others	Caring
To maintain integrity	Wisdom

*Children who learn to trust that their needs will be met have *faith* in their providers. This faith, initially conferred on humans, can eventually be transferred to the One who fills all our human needs.

Resources

Betz, Charles H. *How to Teach the Bible with Power.* Review and Herald, 1995.

Case, Steve. *It's My Choice - Junior Baptismal Guide.* Review and Herald, 1996.

Children's Ministries Department, North American Division. *Coming to Jesus, Growing in Him* booklet. AdventSource, 1992.

Habenicht, Donna. *How to Help Your Child Really Love Jesus.* Review and Herald, 1994.

Habenicht, Donna and Anne Bell. *How to Teach Children in Sabbath School.* Review and Herald, 1983.

Strommen, Merle P. *Four Imperatives: Youth and Family Ministry.* Augsburg Youth and Family Institute, 1991.

5 Learning Styles

Announce a Bible quiz that includes figuring out a coded message, and you immediately have Eric's attention. But you've lost Jennifer, who shrinks down into her chair. However, if you ask for volunteers to act out the Bible story in pantomime, Jennifer can hardly contain herself!

Each person has his or her own "learning style"—their preferred way of dealing with ideas and day-to-day situations. Professionals have divided these into four basic learning styles:
- Innovative Learner
- Analytic Learner
- Common Sense Learner
- Dynamic Learner

Your individual learning style can affect your career choice, how you relate to others, and how you solve problems. Your own learning style can also affect the way you teach.

"There is no right or wrong learning style. It's a matter of which style comes most naturally to you."

—Barbara Manspeaker

Whether learning or teaching, you'll feel most comfortable using your preferred learning style. One of the greatest benefits of

Know Your Style

Directions: Each statement is followed by four possible responses. On a scale of 1 to 4, with 4 being most like you and 1 least like you, rank the responses. Don't use any number more than once per line.

1. As a person, I am
____ **a.** responsive   ____ **b.** a thinker

2. When I tackle a new task
____ **a.** I consider every alternative   ____ **b.** I study up on it

3. When I learn I want
____ **a.** reasons   ____ **b.** facts

4. I tend to be
____ **a.** too soft-hearted   ____ **b.** too dependent on facts and figures

5. I tend to rely on
____ **a.** my feelings   ____ **b.** my judgment

6. I most enjoy in a learning situation
____ **a.** small group discussions   ____ **b.** accuracy and orderliness

7. When faced with problems, I
____ **a.** seek input from peers   ____ **b.** seek logical solutions

8. In choosing solutions, I look for
____ **a.** agreement   ____ **b.** accuracy

9. When I buy, I am most influenced by
____ **a.** the salesperson   ____ **b.** *Consumer Reports*

10. I identify with
____ **a.** caring people   ____ **b.** knowledgeable people

11. I am:
____ **a.** a people person   ____ **b.** a logical person

12. When dealing with new information, I like to:
____ **a.** file it for future use   ____ **b.** analyze it

____ **Total Column 1**   ____ **Total Column 2**

Preferred Learning Style Inventory

© 1993, NAD Church Ministries. *This test was prepared by Dr. Gene Brewer and Noelene Johnsson, and may be photocopied for use in a class or seminar setting. No part of this test may be copied for use in printed form without written permission of the authors.*

____ **c.** practical   ____ **d.** a risk taker

____ **c.** I seek advice from one who has done it   ____ **d.** I start right in and do it my way

____ **c.** involvement   ____ **d.** results

____ **c.** too hasty   ____ **d.** too impulsive

____ **c.** common sense   ____ **d.** my intuition

____ **c.** exploring possible solutions   ____ **d.** self-reliance

____ **c.** seek practical solutions   ____ **d.** act on hunches

____ **c.** efficiency   ____ **d.** predicted results

____ **c.** the test drive plus warranty   ____ **d.** impulse

____ **c.** sensible people—problem solvers, efficient people   ____ **d.** enterprising people

____ **c.** a practical person   ____ **d.** an enthusiastic person

____ **c.** apply it to new situations   ____ **d.** put it to practical use

____ **Total Column 3**   ____ **Total Column 4**

knowing and using the various learning styles is that we are more able to reach ALL of God's children.

So, what is your learning style? To find out your preferred learning style, take the simple learning style inventory on pp. 56-57.

Learning Styles Inventory

The four columns relate to the four learning styles. The column with the highest total is your preferred style. You will discover that you use a combination of several learning styles, though one style usually predominates.

Column 1	Innovative Learner	Style 1
Column 2	Analytic Learner	Style 2
Column 3	Common Sense Learner	Style 3
Column 4	Dynamic Learner	Style 4

Kids with Styles

Do not group your students according to their learning styles.

You do not know for certain what their personal style is. Besides, mixing the various styles enriches the overall learning experience for all members of your class.

The Four Learning Styles

Innovative Learners

Learn by listening and observing. Want reasons to learn.

Strengths: Have imaginative ability. Understand people. Recognize problems. Brainstorm. These people are often the conscience of the group — prophets. They are usually concerned with relationships between people. They will not walk out of a class or meeting for fear of hurting someone's feelings.

Likes: Small group interaction, mimes, role-playing, team sports, simulation. Use in Sabbath School: arts and crafts, creative writing, role plays.

Dislikes: Timed tests, debates, computer-intensive education, lack of artistic expression.

Weaknesses: Files away information instead of acting on it. Reluctant to make decisions. Can be paralyzed by alternatives. Sometimes fails to recognize problems and opportunities.

Learning Question: Answer the question "Why do I need to learn this?" at the start of the lesson so the student will be motivated to learn.

Teaching Tip: Respect their feelings, affirm them, take them into your confidence. Let them know what they are supposed to do and assume they are going to follow through.

Analytic Learners

Learn by abstract conceptualization. They are usually thinkers. Want to learn content.

Strengths: Good at planning, creating models, defining problems and developing theories. They like to reason inductively.

Likes: Programmed instruction, well-organized lectures/stories, competition, demonstrations, objective tests. Use in Sabbath School: quizzes, discussions, abstract Bible studies, personal inventories, coded scriptures and puzzles.

Dislikes: Role-playing, group projects, teachers who don't stay on the task, true/false questions.

Weaknesses: Can be so involved in abstract thinking that they don't make good practical applications. When learning to do something, they may read books and study up on it, but never get around to doing it.

Learning Question: "What do I need to learn?"

Teaching Tip: These learners want direct, no-nonsense communication. Explain the reasons for their assignments and rules and give them an opportunity to explain their reasons for behavior that you might question. Back up your explanation with facts and quotes from experts. Style 2 learners respond well to established routines and rules, particularly if they had a say in establishing them.

Common Sense Learners

Learn through direct hands-on experiences. Want to process the content and apply it to new situations.

Strengths: Good at problem-solving, decision-making, deductive reasoning and applying new ideas to new situations. Likes to help plan a program and carry out instructions with a minimum of adult help.

Likes: Problem-solving, debates, logic problems, independent study, experiments. Use in Sabbath School: experiments, something to make, drama/writing/planning, problems to solve, role-playing involving application of the lesson to everyday life.

Dislikes: Memorizing, reading assignments, group work, writing assignments.

Weaknesses: May solve the wrong problem; may make hasty decisions; have lack of focus, no testing of ideas, scattered thoughts.

Learning Question: "How do I use the information?"

Teaching Tip: They want to get right to the point! Don't give them a long history of the problem or assignment. These learners respond well to time limits. They appreciate knowing that they have your support. Allow them some latitude, some choice in completing your assignment.

Dynamic Learners

Learn by starting right in and doing it. Like to see, hear, touch and feel. Want to use content. Want to produce results.

Strengths: Are result-oriented. Like getting things done. They take leadership, are good at explaining policies, make great salespeople. They take risks. May have to redo the job because they didn't plan sufficiently before starting.

Likes: Case studies, reflective thinking, dramatics, producing creative products, assignments requiring originality, multiple choice and true/false questions. Use in Sabbath School: hands-on activities, real-life simulations, carrying out/producing a drama, planning of real-life events, listing and organizing material.

Dislikes: Seating charts, assignments without options, standard routine, activities done in haste.

Weaknesses: Begins lots of jobs but don't complete them on time. Trivial improvements, meaningless activities. Planning is impractical and not always goal-oriented.

Learning Question: Answer the question "What if?" Get students thinking of other possibilities. Let them teach what they have learned.

Teaching Tip: These students often come across as trying to find a way around your directives. They are looking for a "what-if" opportunity. What if I do it differently? What if I do something else? So be firm. Speak with confidence; be businesslike. And spell out the bottom line—what is the minimum requirement? Then offer contests/rewards as an incentive to challenge them to do more. Expect them to be responsible. Seek their advice or opinion on minor things but insist on that bottom line.

Conventional Wisdom

Learning Alert!

If you are a Style 4 teacher, your intuitive or analytic learners are likely to irritate you. Likewise, if you are an intellectual, traditional Style 2 teacher, you are likely to frustrate Style 4 learners, unless you plan for their learning style.

Learning Styles—So What?

Understanding learning styles helps you make each classroom activity as palatable as possible for all styles. If you mix activities and match activities so as to appeal to different styles you can RELAX. Learners will be happy if at least one activity per class presentation appeals to their learning style.

Finally, learning styles are not meant to predict behavior, attitudes or results. But they do tell us that learners:
- Learn in different ways
- Have varying needs
- Appreciate a choice of activities and approaches
- Need practice using all styles of learning activities

> **Great Idea!**
>
> ## Try This!
> Plan an active family worship around one specific Bible verse. Choose an activity for each learning style. Let everyone choose which activity to do.
>
> For instance: Style 1—create a poster or poem, Style 2—write a prayer or a quiz, Style3—rewrite the verse in today's kid talk, Style 4—role play the verse's meaning.

Resources

Dunn, Rita and Kenneth. *Teaching Elementary Students Through Their Individual Learning Styles.* Allyn & Bacon, 1992.

Johnsson, Noelene. *Learning in Styles: Four Ways People Learn* (video seminar). Advent*Source*, 1996.

Johnsson, Noelene and Suzanne Perdew. "*Preferred Learning Styles.*" Kid's Stuff, Fall, 1994, pp. 6-9.

LeFever, Marlene D. *Learning Styles: Reaching Everyone God Gave You to Teach.* David C. Cook Publishing Company, 1995.

McCarthy, Bernice. *The 4 Mat. System. Teaching to Learning Styles with Right/Left Mode Techniques.* Excel, Inc. 1980, 1987.

Roehlkepartain, Joelene. *Children's Ministry That Works! The Basics and Beyond.* Group Publishing, Inc., 1991.

Newsletters:

Learning Styles Network Newsletter. St. John's University, Grand Central & Utopia Parkways, Jamaica, NY 11439.

Teacher Touch. Marlene LeFever, editor. Elgin, Illinois. David C. Cook Church Ministries.

6 Modes of Learning

All of us learn through our senses. Our brains process information provided by our eyes, ears, nose, tongue, and touch sensors. Just as we each possess a preferred learning style or way of perceiving and dealing with ideas, so we also have a favored mode or vehicle of learning—visual (sight), auditory (sound), kinesthetic (touch) or experiential (experiencing). In a specific learning situation, a person will prefer to use one of the four modes.

The lecture-style class assumes that all prefer the auditory mode. Actually, most people prefer the visual mode over the auditory. They want to see instead of just listening. Others may prefer to touch and feel or even to learn by experiencing and solving real life problems.

"The more we understand ourselves and our own mode of learning, the better equipped we will be to teach others."

—Barbara Manspeaker

Most learners do not use one mode exclusively but different modes in different learning situations. For instance, a child may learn a memory verse best when hearing it said or sung many times. However, the same person may prefer to study the lesson by reading it from the quarterly.

Everyone has one mode that tends to be dominant. A person pursues that mode in most learning situations because it is the

Finding Your Preferred Learning Mode

Directions: Discover your own preferred mode of learning. Circle the letter for the response you would enjoy most.

1. I would prefer to
    a. Listen to a story on tape
    b. Watch a story on video
    c. Prepare a special contribution that kids put on for adults
    d. Make something to illustrate a story

2. When I learn something new, I want to
    a. Hear someone explain it
    b. Read the text for myself
    c. Use the information in real life
    d. Touch the real thing and maybe take it apart

3. When assembling something the first time, I usually need only to
    a. Hear someone describe what to do
    b. See a picture or diagram
    c. Read the directions one step at a time as I fit the pieces together
    d. Figure out what to do by fitting the parts together

4. I prefer a lecturer to
    a. Tell the various points she is making without interruption
    b. Demonstrate the points she is making so I can see what she is talking about
    c. Let me get involved with solving a real problem and then make the main points in the context of the problem
    d. Use models and objects to make the point and let me hold them

5. My favorite learning activity involves
    a. Listening to audio tapes
    b. Watching a video
    c. Planning and preparing a TV show
    d. Making a craft

6. If I need to learn how to get somewhere, I
    a. Ask someone to tell me the best way to go
    b. Ask someone to draw a simple map
    c. Get a map, start out, and maybe ask if I get lost
    d. Ask or read the directions and draw my own map

What is Your Mode?

If you scored 6 of one letter, you undoubtedly prefer the learning style listed beside that letter below; 4-5 indicates a probable preference for that style; 1-3 indicates you do not show a strong preference for that style. If your scores were distributed among the three or four styles, you are a multi-sensory learner and like to use all modes.

   a. auditory mode
   b. visual mode
   c. experiential learner
   d. kinesthetic learner

most comfortable and productive. Students learn best and enjoy learning the most when they are learning in the mode for which they have a preference.

Understanding the Modes

In describing the first three modes we could simply say: the visual learner wants to see, the auditory learner wants to hear, and the kinesthetic learner must touch. The experiential learner, on the other hand, gets totally involved in the process of accomplishing a task, often using all three modes simultaneously as she experiences the learning concept in a more practical way.

Hearing, seeing, and touching involve the senses, but the experiential mode involves more; it puts learning into a real life context, thus giving experiential learning a distinction of its own.

We should not categorize any child into a single learning mode. Instead, we should encourage them to try additional ways of comprehending and absorbing knowledge.

Learning Takes Place When...

- Visual learners are encouraged to observe something from all angles.
- Kinesthetic learning takes place when we allow children to handle and manipulate something from which they can learn.
- Experiential learning occurs when a student wants to take the object apart to understand how it works or goes together.
- Auditory learning takes place when a child picks up a working model and listens to the sound it makes as well as when the student listens to the teacher's answers to student questions. Auditory learning also takes place when students listen to other students describe what they will make, tell what they have made, or what they learned from an activity.

Using the Modes to Give Directions

Mode	Use When...
Auditory	Giving routine directions
	Signaling a transition
	Giving directions at a self-directed learning center.
Visual	Explaining a procedure
Kinesthetic	Learning the steps in a process
Experiential	Kids begin unassisted activities and projects.

Example

Moving to an activity center, say: "It's time to go (wherever)." Tell who goes where.

When it's time for young children to sing, pray, clean up, etc., use a song as the cue. The song introduces the required actions.

Record simple directions on audio tape. Leave in a tape player ready for non-readers to play. At the end of your instructions, tell the user how to rewind and play the tape again.

When giving instructions for individual or small group activities, have the directions written out for the students to read. Or for non-readers, draw a picture for each step; number the steps. Or demonstrate the procedure so all can see.

Students work along with the teacher. Tell them the next step when they have completed the previous step. Students then do the whole process.

The students may be told the expected outcome (e.g. to make a pyramid) but not how to. They figure out a procedure as they accomplish the task. (In so doing, they learn creativity, organizational skills, etc.)*

*Note: When students assist in routine tasks, such as assembling and passing out supplies, they are engaged in experiential learning. Cooperation, service, and responsibility are the by-product.

Alive in a Fiery Furnace

You can tell the story of Shadrach, Meshach, and Abednego using all the modes of learning!

Visual: Replace the light bulb in your primary classroom with a red light bulb before children arrive. This will create a fiery glow as though they are entering a fiery furnace.

Auditory: Give each child a sheet of stiff cellophane paper. As you tell the story, have them crinkle their paper to make the sounds of crackling fire.

Kinesthetic: Have kids tell stories about times they touched something very hot, such as a stove. Ask them what happened and how it felt.

Experiential: Pour Liquid Smoke (available at grocery stores) into a bowl and have children dip their fingers into it before you tell the story. As you tell the story, have them smell their fingers and imagine what it might have smelled like in the fiery furnace.

Visual Learners

Who they are. Visual learners approach learning through the eyes. These people see pictures in their heads. The pictures help them to understand and remember. They visualize a Bible event, "seeing" the scene and action as the story is told or read. This helps it become a permanent memory. Imagination enhances the visual learning process. Because visual learners "see" the scene in their minds, they remember what the scenes "look" like. A typical visual learner tends to be good at both observing details and remembering them.

What they say. The visual learner is likely to use the following phrases frequently in conversation:

"Guess what I saw!"
"Look at it this way..."
"Picture it..."
"Do you see..."
"I see..."
"Show me..."
"It looks like ..."

Identifying characteristics. Visual learners are likely to choose a seat where they can see all that is going on. They feel frustrated if they can't see and tend to have a shorter attention span for activities that are not enhanced by visual aids. They will ask you to repeat directions over and over unless they can read them.

Ways to teach visual learners. Paint word pictures when you must speak without visual aids. Explain the unseen by comparing it to something familiar. Provide details of size, shape, and color. Any of the following are helpful for visual learners:
- Felts or pictures to illustrate a story
- Object lessons
- Dramatizations, skits, or role play
- Videos or films
- Illustrated songbooks for teaching songs
- Illustrated poems
- Diagrams, time lines, charts and graphs for older children
- Maps to help locate places
- Decorations that enhance what you teach - banners, posters, photographs
- Flip charts, black/white boards or overheads to record key words
- Overhead transparencies for pictures, silhouettes or writing
- Displays and dioramas to teach mission, Bible settings, and nature
- Printed directions for activities, such as crafts
- Drawings that illustrate steps in a procedure

Try This...

Teach this week's Sabbath School lesson (or an Adventurer Club lesson) using three of the visuals listed above. When the lesson is done, ask the students what they learned and how they felt about the activities. Try to determine whether or not the children are visual learners.

Auditory Learners

Who they are. Auditory learners are like tape recorders. Their minds record what they hear and also process the information and remember it. Auditory learners often hear sounds, such as voice inflections and word parts, more acutely than others. Generally, they hear it once and remember. Verbal directions are no problem; they don't care in the least whether they are written down or illustrated. Their mental cassette tapes are generally long enough to remember everything they need to know and they generally have good verbalization skills. Sound effects accompanying a presentation are very effective and enjoyable for them.

What they say. The auditory learner may use the following phrases frequently:
"I hear..."
"It sounds like..."
"Listen to..."
"It says..."
"Something tells me..."
"Tell me..."
"I'd like to hear..."
"Describe what..."

Identifying characteristics. The auditory learner will tend to sit in the back of a classroom because listening is enough for them. They are the ones most likely to "listen" to what the teacher says. When teaching new songs, they need to listen three to four times before singing the song.

Ways to teach auditory learners. Any of the following activities are likely to be effective with auditory learners.
- Brainstorming ideas
- Debates and simulated committees where they take a position and defend it
- Audio cassettes to listen to and to record themselves
- Choral readings or responsive readings

- Oral quizzes
- Songs that teach, such as Psalm 23 or Books of the Bible
- Play a game identifying sounds
- Guided discussions in which they answer questions and share opinions
- Memory verses set to music (they may even fit a verse to music)
- Tell stories or give a talk
- Listening games
- Oral reports of research, trips, experiences
- Radio/TV interviews, newscasts, talk shows as on-the-spot simulations
- Scenarios they complete by telling the outcome or giving advice
- Skits where they have a speaking part

Great Idea! Try This...
Play a story tape for students which they have never heard. When it is over, quiz the children on what they heard and learned. Try to identify your auditory learners.

Kinesthetic Learners

Who they are. Kinesthetic learners are hands-on people. These are the "muscle" people. The physical and the mental team up together to help the student learn, to give meaning and purpose to knowledge. As she handles, creates, or takes apart something, her brain is processing the information and memorizing. Her small-motor skills, such as writing and cutting with scissors, develop somewhat earlier than average. She finds enjoyment in coloring, cutting, pasting, and writing. She may have trouble following directions and will become restless and inattentive during long inactive sessions.

What they say. The kinesthetic learner may use the following feeling words or phrases frequently:

"It feels..."
"I'm in touch with..."

"It rubs me..."
"How do you feel about..."
"Let me examine..."
"May I touch..."
"May I play..."
"May I handle..."
"I made..."
"May I make..."

Learning characteristics. This learner often chooses to sit close to the action so as not to miss any opportunity to touch. She will ask to color, cut, paste, write, take it apart and may sometimes simply sit and touch.

Try This...
Ask students to write a story, draw a picture, or make something that shows Jesus' love for them. Try to identify your kinesthetic learners.

Ways to teach kinesthetic learners. Use some of the following activities according to the developmental stage of the learner:
- Creative writing projects, such as stories, poems, news stories
- Craft projects including mobiles, balloon art, and modeling with clay
- Activity sheets on the lesson
- Word puzzles, such as coded messages, seek a word, acrostics, etc.
- Diagrams, maps, and cartoons that students make
- Collages to cut and paste
- Interviews, surveys, and evaluations they do
- Research in the Bible, concordance, dictionary, and atlas with written reports
- Written tests
- Posters they make in groups
- Art projects
- Jigsaw and other manipulative puzzles
- Graffiti boards they take charge of
- Lists to make

The Experiential Learner

Who they are. Students who like to be involved in practical, real life situations. These are the children who like to use a combination of learning modes to achieve something practical. They get totally involved in the learning process. They receive satisfaction from fixing things without help and like to do practical things correctly. One may offer to clean up and put away; another, to make and serve snacks. If the class is doing a skit or play, these are the people who pull the curtains, run the sound system, make and sell tickets, and maybe even direct the play.

Ways to teach experiential learners. Involve them in class projects and situations such as the following:
- Religious TV shows the kids prepare and maybe even videotape themselves
- Creative dramatics, such as skits, role plays, and charades
- Game show simulations
- Hands-on service projects
- Field trips
- Group projects
- Nursing home, hospital, or shut-in visits
- Prayer bands, prayer journals
- Fund raisers for missions, either local or foreign
- Interactive stories with dramatization and sound effects
- Life simulating games
- Programs for adults, such as open house at their Sabbath School

"We should seek to make learning both experiential and multi-sensory in approach as often as possible."
—Barbara Manspeaker

Planning Multi-sensory, Active Learning for All Modes

Multi-sensory learning provides activities and experiences for all modes of learning so students can learn the way they prefer. To teach an effective Bible lesson, the teacher need not identify each child's preferred mode. Instead, the teacher plans learning activities making sure each mode is favored in at least one activity.

For example, when teaching young children the story of Christ's birth, the children might listen (auditory mode) to the story and at the same time see (visual mode) a picture of it. They might help to act out the Bible story (experiential mode) before they listen (auditory mode) to a memory verse song tape. Finally they will make (kinesthetic mode) a memory verse bookmark to take home and share (experiential mode) with a neighbor.

Educators recommend a multi-sensory, active learning environment to help children use all their available modes of learning—a challenge to every Children's Ministries leader and teacher!

Great Idea! Try This...

Get a copy of Linnea Torkelsen's, *Who Cares? A Zillion Ways You Can Meet the Needs of People Around You* (Advent*Source*). This little book contains dozens of service projects that have been adult approved and kid tested! They are a great way to let kids experience service. Choose a project that matches the unique gifts in your local group and follow through to the completion of the project in a live setting.

Resources

Case, Steve and Fred Cornforth. *Hands-On Service Ideas for Youth Groups.* Group Publishing, 1996.

Torkelsen, Linnea. *Who Cares? A Zillion Ways You Can Meet the Needs of People Around You.* Advent*Source*, 1996.

7 Understanding Active Learning

"OK, there's a child that sits in your Sabbath School or Pathfinder class that begins to irritate the daylights out of all the other children. They begin to distract, punch or kick to get attention and you're saying: 'Johnnie, be still, dear. Johnnie...Johnnie, now listen....'

And because you had to keep talking to him, by the end of class, you're ready to string him up by his toenails. Have you had this experience?

"Many times I work with teachers who come in and say they are doing the same things with children they were doing in the 50's or 60's. Somehow they don't seem able to manage. The class is falling apart, and they say to me 'Why? I'm not doing anything different than I was when I started. I'm doing the same thing I did back then (in the 60's). How come it's not working now?'

I have to tell them, 'You're dealing in a very different time, and that's exactly your problem. You're not doing anything differently.'"

—Mayra Rodriguez

So we need to teach differently. How different? What are we supposed to do? Before answering that question, we must look closely at how children learn.

Children Remember What They Do

The Sunoco Company sponsored research to study how people learn. They first instructed a group of adults by using a tape recording. Three hours later, the adults could remember 70 percent of what they had heard. But three days later, they could recall only 10 percent of the content.

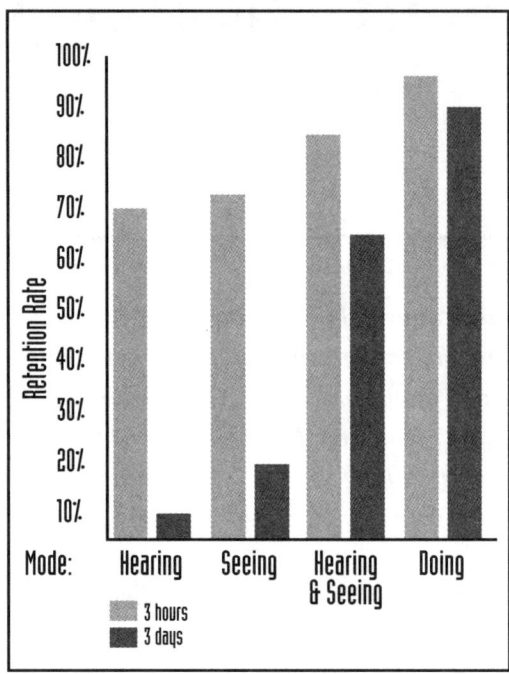

The next learning session involved visual learning only. Three hours later the adults remembered 72 percent of the material; three days later 20 percent.

In the third learning test both hearing and seeing were involved. Three hours later recall was up to 85 percent; 3 days later, 65 percent.

The fourth test involved learning by doing. Immediate recall was 95 percent; after three days, 90 percent.

The study clearly shows that people learn best by doing (experiencing) and least well by listening to a lecture. However, visual aids can dramatically increase the learning value of a lecture. The implications for Children's Ministries are clear:
- There must be less teacher talk and more student participation in learning.
- Teachers should be more like coaches than lecturers.
- The task of the teacher is not to deliver knowledge but to create learning situations for the students.

Sometimes referred to as active, inductive or discovery learning, this style of teaching creates an environment where students are presented with an activity or problem and then engaged in responding to or solving it. Teachers can then guide students through a process of self-discovery.

The Discovery-style Lesson

In discovery learning the teacher has a goal (objective) to help students understand specific Bible truth based on a specific Bible story and scripture texts. Having clearly understood the objective, the teacher plans activities that will help students explore the meaning of the scripture.

The object of the discovery learning activities is to help prepare kids' minds for the concept you want them to understand, or to familiarize them with the text. The activities may also help kids to relate the lesson to their own life experience.

When each activity is completed, the teacher debriefs the student by asking questions about what the student learned. Sometimes what the kids learn is quite different from what the teacher had in mind. Knowing this helps the teacher to either carry on in the direction the kids are headed, or to focus them in another direction.

How to Make Active Learning Work

In order for students to learn from an activity, they must have clear directions, the necessary materials, a chance to do the activity, and a chance to discuss what they learned.

Giving Directions

Giving directions is an art that can be learned with practice. Clear directions use simple language, and break down the task into steps. Good directions spell out the steps in the order they will be followed. The directions can be written on construction paper and taped up where everyone can read them, or the teacher

Healing the Centurion's Servant: Discovery Learning Activities

The following readiness activities are designed to help children understand the Centurion's faith in the healing of the his servant, in Matthew 8:5-13. (You would probably use only one of them in your lesson.)

Making Cottage Cheese. (Kindergarten/Primary)

Give 1/4 cup of warm milk and a half lemon to each student. Remind the kids that when babies are hungry, they are fed milk. Ask why they are given a drink when they need to eat. If babies could talk they might even object—just as kids their age do when they don't understand why parents do something. Tell the kids to squeeze the lemon juice into the milk, stir it, and see what happens (the milk thickens). Collect their milk in a pan and show some cottage cheese. Explain that if they were to slowly heat the thickened milk in a pan, it would turn into cottage cheese.

To debrief. Ask if cottage cheese is a drink or a food (a food). Explain that milk undergoes a similar change in a baby's stomach. Read Matthew 8:10. Ask how do babies demonstrate faith when they are hungry? (They drink the milk.) How do children demonstrate faith at mealtime? (They eat.) When they pray? (They believe God hears and answers.) How is faith like trust? (It's the same.)

Faith in a Bottle. (Juniors)

Give 3 or 4 volunteers identical spoons and the same amount of water, dry rice or beans. Give each a different container: a jug with a small neck, a half-liter pop bottle, a half-gallon milk carton, or a large pan. Tell them you want to see who will be first, at the starting signal, to empty all their water (rice or beans) into their container and put the empty container up-side-down on their head. Set up the race and appoint the other kids to judge the winners, noting if the contents are spilled.

---

can give the steps one at a time, waiting for everyone to complete a step before telling the next one. The more mature the student, the more independently they like to work and the more important to have directions written out. If directions are given orally, the students are likely to ask for the directions be told over and over again.

Providing Materials

Providing materials can be greatly facilitated by keeping supplies of much-used materials on hand in the classroom. Materials

To debrief. Ask the contestants to tell how they felt about the race. (It was fun—for the winner, OK, unfair for others). Ask the person with the pop bottle to tell why she thought it unfair. (The narrow neck slowed her down.) Ask them how construction on a highway can cause a bottleneck at rush hour. How did the busy centurion try to prevent a bottleneck in Matthew 8:8? (If Jesus just said the word, it would save Him a lot of time and all the other people would not have to wait to be healed.) How was the centurion's suggestion an act of faith? (He believed Jesus had the power to heal by just giving the command.)

Starfish Faith. (Primary)

Have the children twice fold in half a 3" square of industrial strength, brown paper towel. Using the only pair of scissors available, cut a deep V as shown. They then open out the starfish and fold back each arm, its tip over the center. They drop the folded starfish in a pan of water, watching the arms unfold. Tell them you want to see who can make the most starfish in 3-4 minutes. The object is to create a frustrating bottleneck so that the children in their frustration, suggest you get more scissors.

To debrief. After a while, gather the kids and talk about how they felt (mad, slow, sad, frustrated) and why. (They wanted to get the most, but had to wait.) Tell the kids that as you read Matthew 8:5-13 they should look for similarities and differences in their situation and that of the centurion. (There is no bottleneck; Jesus takes the centurion's advice where you did not take theirs.) Ask what if a multitude of sick or homeless people had suddenly surrounded Jesus. What would have happened to the centurion? (He would have to wait.)

Try This...

Choose one of these activities to try with your class.

most often used include: pens, pencils, crayons, markers, scissors, glue, typing paper, construction paper, newspaper, cotton balls, yarn and string. Keep baskets or boxes of supplies for each class group in an easily accessible place; students can quickly get and distribute them for you.

Doing the Activity

A chance to do the activity is safeguarded when children are supplied materials and instructions and then allowed to carry

them out alone or with a friend. Teachers, acting as coaches, stand ready to offer suggestions when needed. Remember:
- Don't do the activity for the kids.
- Allow children flexibility (there is more than one way to do an activity). Affirm students for their creativity and the uniqueness of their finished product.

Debriefing the Activity

Debrief the students by discussing what was learned. This is the best way to ensure that learning has taken place. To debrief the students, do the following in the order given:
- Question the students as to how they feel about the activity.
- Ask them what they learned about the Bible text or the main idea you are teaching.

For students to get the main idea of an activity, the teacher needs to focus learning to that idea and articulate it. If the same idea comes out in more than one activity, the students are more likely to remember it. The best remembered lessons are those in which all the learning activities and the lesson center around one idea.

Try This...

Based on the descriptions given above, write student directions for the activities. Then try them out on a group of students. When the students are done with the activity, evaluate your direction-giving skills as follows:
- **Great**—students did as you expected without asking you to explain what the directions meant.
- **Good**—students asked only once for clarification.
- **So-so**—two or more points of the directions had to be clarified.
- **Uh-oh!**—they continually asked for clarification

Bible Learning Activities

Bible learning activities (BLAs) are just what the name implies—activities that help kids learn about the Bible. Each word of the generic title "Bible learning activity" has special meaning, as illustrated by the statements below that qualify each word of the title. BLAs are meant to lead students into the Word.

Bible

The word "Bible" is not tacked on as a buzz word indicating an activity approved for Sabbath.
- BLAs are designed with a specific Bible text or story in mind.
- The goal of the activity is to help kids better understand the text.
- When the activity is completed, the students are asked to read the text.
- The students explain how the activity helps them understand the text.

"Sometimes activities fail or fizzle. One cannot always predict or prevent disaster, but the creative teacher learns to go with the flow. Echo the feelings of the students. Groan or laugh when they do, recovering quickly to turn the disaster into a learning situation. Ask what they learned from the situation; follow up on their line of thought."

—Noelene Johnsson

Learning

BLAs are for learning, not for entertainment. Nevertheless…
- Learning should be enjoyable.
- When evaluating an activity for its learning value, ask:
    Did real learning take place? What did the students learn?

Activities

Activities imply that kids are deeply involved in what goes on…
- They do something in order to discover more about a concept. When teaching with activities:
    - Plan to involve all of the senses in the course of the lesson.
    - Help kids experience a concept.
- Use pencil and paper activities as a way to process prior experiences. Activity sheets are particularly useful when they encourage kids to look inside themselves.

"Activities aren't over when they are done. Discussion needs to follow an activity; discussion helps to "cement" the learning process. Discussion is not the activity."

—Jerry Bartram

Using Bible Learning Activities

BLAs can be used to make any part of a lesson or program active: mission, prayer, singing, memory work, Bible story, lesson readiness, lesson application. Children do not need every part of the program or lesson to be made active.

Activities can be done in large groups or small. Ideally, everyone should have a chance to get involved in an activity. But if the room is too crowded and the activity requires movement, you might have a group come up and do the activity while the others watch. Then involve everyone in a discussion of the activity, huddling in tight groups with their teachers to answer your questions. Be sure to give each group a chance to report their group's conclusions.

Conventional Wisdom

Activities do not have to be completed for learning to take place. Some students will want to stay and finish craft-type activities after class or they can finish them at home.

Readiness Activities

Readiness activities prepare the mind for the main idea of the lesson; they precede the Bible study, connecting the students with something they already know about the subject. Readiness activities help students activate the appropriate file drawer of their mind's knowledge and past experiences. Unless they put the new information in context, students may not know how to apply the Bible truth they learn.

Typical readiness activities involve students in activities such as the following:
- Remembering an early experience relevant to the new concept
- Doing an interview to ask someone else about related experiences
- Finding examples of related experiences in a newspaper or magazine
- Rating themselves on skills related to the concept
- Discovering Bible texts that relate to the concept
- Guessing definitions of the concept
- Finding definitions or facts in dictionary, encyclopedia, or maps

The three "Healing the Centurion's Servant" activities described above were all designed as readiness activities.

Application Activities

After studying the Bible lesson, we use application activities to help the students make practical use of the new Bible truth. Role plays, simulated committee meetings, board meetings, and elections can help students relate what they learned to real life. One of the best application activities involves setting up a scenario—a setting in which somebody has a problem. Kids figure out their advice for solving the problem. For example:

Simon's Struggle Scenario. Simon's mother died after a brief but painful illness. Simon, his brother, and their dad are devastated. Simon wants to know why God took his mother. How could your knowledge of God's love help Simon? What might you say to him?

The scenario idea can be expanded into an activity where kids get involved in detailed planning for an imaginary situation. For instance, they can imagine themselves given the charge of bringing up a 3-year-old and make lists of what they would buy the child for his diet, clothing, recreation, and education. After the kids report their plans and get excited about the child, tell them of a temptation that has come to the child. Ask them to tell how their plans would have helped the child prepare for the temptation. (Probably they would be of little help. Realizing their omission, students suddenly understand why their parents make some of the rules they do.)

Types of Bible Learning Activities

- **Artistic Activities**

    Activities that allow artistic expression involve kids in making things like posters, collages, booklets, greeting cards, pictures and sculptures using different materials. Also carvings, crafts, models, etc.

- **Creative Writing Activities**

    Writing letters, invitations, poems, songs, greeting cards, news reports, stories, resumes, advertisements, scripts, paraphrasing Bible verses and retelling stories in a modern setting are typical creative writing activities. Tip: Some students dislike creative writing, so give them the option of planning the ideas and telling them to you or the group, or allow them to work with a partner.

- **Dramatized Activities**

    These activities allow kids to express themselves by acting out a parts, e.g. skits, charades, plays, motion songs and verses, role playing and any form of reenactment.

- **Research Activities**

    Research activities typically involve kids in study and searching out information. Examples are: dictionary use, concordance or map studies, Bible searches, newspaper checks, looking up statistics, and perhaps surveys.

Use activity sheets sparingly.

- **Puzzles and Games**

    Rebuses, word puzzles, coded texts, and a variety of word games can be used for learning purposes. When games from childhood are resurrected for a learning purpose, the object is not in playing or winning, but in discovering something new and unexpected.

- **Experiential Activities**

When kids do something for the sake of experiencing a given situation, we call it an experiential activity. This category might include: life simulations, experiments, physical exercise or manipulation, relays, hunts, surveys, etc.

Conventional Wisdom

Using Games as a Learning Tool

Games have a limited use in learning. The competitive aspect of many games, such as Bible baseball, make them popular with some kids, but kids can become so obsessed with winning that learning is crowded out.

Non-competitive games, however, are useful in teaching rote learning and in reviewing facts. But care needs to be taken lest the game trivializes the material being learned or reviewed.

Bible Learning Centers

Learning centers are learning situations, set up so small groups of children can learn by self-directed Bible learning activities or under the supervision of a teacher. The teacher explains the directions for young children in terms of what the group is doing. (We are making a road for Jesus to ride His donkey.) Older students, however, read and follow the directions without help. Learning centers contribute to the objectives of the lesson. The learning may be debriefed later, after the entire class has a chance to get involved.

Any traditional program can be broken down into learning centers. The various program components can each be done at a different learning center. Ideally the children are given an opportunity to choose which learning center to join. They rotate around the centers, spending 5-7 minutes at each.

At each center, students are involved in an age-appropriate Bible learning activity, individual activity sheets, making something, or solving a problem. (For example, the "Healing the Centurion's Servant" activities described earlier could each be set up at a different learning center.)

After students have rotated around the centers for 35-40 minutes, they come together as a large group for worship. At the appropriate time, the teacher asks the students to tell what they learned at each center, weaving their experiences at the center into a Bible study about the lesson.

Resources

Many books of Bible learning activities are available. While the program helps for Children's Ministries often suggest BLAs, sometimes they do not fit your needs or interests. That's when you will appreciate having some resources on hand to consult. The following are recommended for your personal or church library.

Christian Crafts from Egg Cartons. Shining Star, 1991.
Christian Crafts from Paper Plates. Shining Star, 1989.
Christian Crafts-Paper Bag Puppets. Shining Star, 1990.
Cornforth, Fred and Kelly Blue Cornforth. *Creative Bible Learning Activities for Junior Teens - 101 Ideas for Junior Teen Leaders.* AdventSource, 1995.
Haystead, Wes. *Design for Teaching Young Children.* Standard Publishing, 1992.
How To Do Bible Learning Activities, Ages 2-5. Gospel Light, 1995.
How To Do Bible Learning Activities, Grades 1-6. Gospel Light, 1995.
Opitz, Dr. Michael F. *Learning Centers, Grades K-4.* Scholastic Professional Books. (The twelve introductory pages provide excellent information about organizing learning centers.)

8 Organizing Your Ministry Program

You have been elected to leadership as a Children's Ministries coordinator in your church and you sincerely want to accomplish something for the Lord, for the children, and for your church. You want to succeed in this endeavor and God wants you to succeed. So at the outset make Him your partner and seek His guidance.

If you are a common sense learner, you probably have the need to jump right in solving problems. If you are a dynamic learner you probably want to start achieving your goals, even if you have not thought them through yet. If you happen to be a visual learner, you may want to start in buying visual aids; if a kinesthetic learner, you itch to make aids or to redecorate Sabbath School rooms.

But if you truly want to succeed and find fulfillment, don't do anything until you get organized. The following steps can help organize your ministry.

Developing a Children's Ministries Plan

Children's Ministries coordinators are entrusted to care for the overall Children's Ministries program in your church. The following straightforward steps can help you plan an effective children's ministry for your church:

1. Look at the big picture
2. Develop an overall plan

3. Resource your ministry plan
4. Publicize your ministry
5. Work your plan
6. Plan for succession

Step 1: Look at the Big Picture

The big picture for Children's Ministries includes an under girding system for getting things done and a superstructure of existing ministries, programs, and systems. These have grown over the years and are largely unmapped. You discover them the hard way, by experience, or you seek a mentor, an elder or deacon, who will help you find your way around the church power structures and explain how things work.

Existing church politics

Politics means the way people of different interests and concerns work together to achieve their goals. In your local church certain people have the power to get things done; their word goes. Find out who these key people are. Discover their goals before talking to them about yours. Emphasize the concerns you have in common. Listen to their advice. Your church also has committees set up to help keep the ministries running smoothly. The church board is the granddaddy of them all. Find out which other committees relate to your ministry. When a committee votes their support for a children's project, the finance committee will take your request for a budget more seriously. Learning how things get done in your church will pay off later when your plans are in place.

Comprehensive church plans

If your church has more than one pastor, chances are the church has a comprehensive plan and goals for ministry and mission. Existing plans can help you identify your ministry niche. If your church has no such plan, you are free to develop your own. If a plan already exists, ask to read it. In the event the church has developed a slogan that sums up their mission, echo that slogan in your plan. For instance, if your church has targeted a new neighborhood to reach or if they plan a major evangelistic event, they will want to support a children's event, such as Vacation Bible School or Neighborhood Bible Camp that will help achieve their goal.

Systems of accountability

Find out to whom you are accountable and who is accountable to you. Generally the Children's Ministries coordinator is accountable to the church board. The Sabbath School council coordinates ministries, develops common ministry goals, and facilitates routine problem solving. It is not, however, meant to be another board that tells you what you may and may not do in Children's Ministries.

The church clerk or Sabbath School secretary may need certain information from you that is required in reporting. They usually keep track of membership, attendance, and offering totals. The children's coordinator needs to appoint someone to keep track of names, ages, addresses, and birthdays.

Leaders of the various Children's Ministries report to the Children's Ministries coordinator who represents them on the church board. Teachers and other helpers are accountable to leaders of the ministry in which they teach. The leaders represent them on the Children's Ministries committee.

Begin right away to build bridges between you and the various levels of accountability. You may need the advice that committees and experienced leaders can give. Listening now can earn you their support when you need votes later.

Determining boundaries

Just as building good fences makes for good neighbors, so identifying ministry overlap and setting boundaries can make for good relationships in ministry.

The established boundaries for Children's Ministries are set in terms of the audience—children ages birth through eighth grade. However, youth, Sabbath School, stewardship, personal ministries, family ministries and church school all have programs for this age span.

The important thing here is not the fence separating the ministries, but the flock—the children.

"Being part of a team that is working for the salvation of children can energize leaders. Working alone and waging turf wars in the end is always counterproductive."

—Noelene Johnsson

The Children's Ministries coordinator needs to bring overlapping ministries together to talk about their goals, coordinate their efforts, and develop a calendar of events for the next twelve months.

Highlighting common goals, mutual respect, and cooperation can eliminate negative competition between ministries.

Existing ministries for children

To fill out the big picture of Children's Ministries at your church, list the ministries now provided by your church. The typical church offers four or five ministries over the course of one year. The more ministries your church offers, the more attractive your church will be to families with children and the more likely your church will grow. Compare what you now offer with the following list:

Adventurer club	Eager Beaver
Baptismal class	Junior/Earliteen heritage tour
Children's bulletins	Junior mentoring
Children's choir	Neighborhood Bible Camp
Children's campmeeting	Neighborhood Bible club
Children's church	Pathfinder club
Children's communion	Sabbath School
Children's evangelistic meetings	Summer day camp
Children's lesson/story in church	Summer ministries interns
Children's prayer meeting	Teen volunteers
Children's tithing	Vacation Bible School
Church nursery	VBS follow-up

Step 2: Overall Plan

Having surveyed the possibilities for ministry, begin thinking about your dreams for your ministry. How much might your ministry accomplish for your church? How much would you be willing and able to do? Whom do you need on your team that will help you accomplish your plan?

Building a team

The leaders of existing Children's Ministries in your church make up the Children's Ministries council. Include an elder, the church treasurer, and the Sabbath School superintendent, if she or he still coordinates children's Sabbath Schools in your church. Take a list of council members to the church board, requesting their vote of approval. The council meets once or twice per quarter, or more often if necessary. Continually remind the council its function is to facilitate and encourage ministry, not to sit in judgment or to restrict service.

Conventional Wisdom

Team Building

- Do work for unity on the team and between Children's Ministries and all other ministries.
- Don't seek a team decision and then go contrary to it.
- Do give equal voice to all members of the council.
- Don't seek advice always or continually make plans with the same people to the exclusion of others.
- Don't do all the talking at council meetings; listen to the team.
- Don't cancel scheduled meetings or turn up late.
- Do delegate and hold the persons responsible for tasks delegated to them.

Gaining buy-in from the team

The secret of successful team building is to have every member buy into the team's plans. This is easier said than done. Once a leader floats an idea, she must be willing to stand back and let the team try to sink it. If the idea has merit and has been well thought out, members of the team will gradually see the light. However, just because a plan is voted down does not mean the plan is necessarily a bad one. Chances are the team needed more time to get used to it or that the leader needed more time to work it out. Maybe the team needed to be in on the idea much sooner.

Develop a shared vision

Envision the plan successfully operating two years from now. What would you like to see and hear? Write a word picture of your vision, using phrases such as, "I see…, I hear…, I feel…."

Share your vision with your mentor, a close supporter, and then at a special meeting of the Children's Ministries council. Encourage the group to react by either writing their own visions or by telling what pleases them about your vision and what troubles them. Together rewrite the vision and develop some goals that will form the basis of a Children's Ministries plan for the next two years. Write more goals than you can accomplish. Then prioritize the goals. Ask everyone to vote the goals of their preference. Vote three times, assigning 6 points per person, as follows: 3 points for their first choice, 2 for the second, and 1 for their third. Before the voting begins, remind them you will give highest priority in terms of budget and time in the order the goals are voted.

Determine goals

Distinguishing between goals and objectives is important. Goals are like destinations—places where you want your ministry to go. Objectives are steps you take to reach the destination. For instance, if you were going to Bombay (your goal), buying a ticket would be an important step (objective) that supports your goal. Goals in Children's Ministries might include any of the following:
- Develop a ministry characterized by grace
- Each ministry will be service-oriented
- Your Children's Ministries will be known in the community for caring and excellence
- Developing an after-school care program
- Making all church programs child-friendly
- Training earliteens and youth to work with children

Develop objectives

One at a time, consider the goals your committee prioritizes. Brainstorm ways to achieve the goal. For instance, to saturate Children's Ministries with grace, you can develop programs that teach unconditional love, plan a workshop to train leaders on ways to demonstrate unconditional acceptance, work with the pastor or the young adult class to plan a weekend or a special church service that celebrates grace, and begin collecting resources on the subject. You might even offer to try out the new Sabbath School curriculum that emphasizes grace.

Action plans

Action plans are all the steps you will take to make an objective happen. For instance, steps to develop a program on unconditional love or how to organize a workshop.

Plan strategies for overcoming difficulties

For each action plan, list all the difficulties you are likely to encounter in pursuing the goal. Then make plans (strategies) for overcoming the difficulties. For example, in giving more prominence to grace, you will upset people who fear that the children will not be taught Christian behavior or who are more comfortable talking about works. You need to find ways to reassure them. Be up-front explaining that changed behavior will not be overlooked; it will be taught as a response to grace, and it will be motivated by grace. Whenever planning for change, you need to warm the atmosphere. Build firmly on the past; keep thanking people for the strong foundation on which you and your team are building.

Step 3: Resource Your Ministry Plan

Think big

People are accomplishing some wonderful things for children. People who are struggling to make a living still find ways to run dynamic and lively ministries for their children and plan outreach programs for huge numbers of community children. How do they do it? They think big. Their success is explained by the talents in Matthew 25:14-30.

Plan for success

In the parable of the talents, a master entrusts various amounts of money to each of his servants. You know the story: The man with the least buries it; the man with the most doubles it. The master, upon his return, chastises the one-talent servant for failing to use and thus increase what he has. The unproductive talent is stripped away from him and given to the servant who has the most, because he will put it to best use. So it is with funds for ministry. God will provide all that leaders can use wisely.

It is a mistake to assume that their is no money for Children's Ministries. Money flows to ideas."

—Debra Brill

Get wise

God is extravagant with His gifts and blessings, but He is not wasteful. He is tirelessly forgiving of our shortcomings, but He isn't foolish. Our God of abundant resources is patiently waiting for us to get a sense of ministry, to become partners in ministry, and to develop a plan. He expects us to practice good stewardship, gaining the most we can for the dollar. If we do these things in accordance with His guidance, we can trust Him to provide the resources—personnel, finances and materials.

Develop people resources

Before you develop the financial budget, try to visualize staffing needs in terms of how many volunteers you need for both existing and new programs. People and time are donated resources; churches should keep track of them. Doing so lets people know the church understands and values their commitment. Congregations should more often give thanks to God for these donated resources. If you have staffing problems, remember God can fill all your needs. Check out Chapter 12 - Staffing Children's Ministries for more information, and keep trusting God to match the person with the need. Don't overlook non-member neighbors and VBS friends who might be glad to help out with a cutting-edge ministry.

"The quality of the programs a church provides is more important than the number of programs. The quality can only be maintained if there is adequate staff. Programs poorly run send a negative message to children, parents and volunteers."

—Barbara Manspeaker

Empower volunteers

Remember how energized and empowered you were when you first took over leadership of a ministry and realized it was up to you to make it as successful as you liked? Try now to pass on this sense of fulfillment to volunteers. Share the need with them; seek their input for working the plan. Give them a chance to say which parts of the plan they will take responsibility for. Then turn over that responsibility and hold them accountable. Remember, empowered volunteers will accomplish way more for you than helpers who help with one job at a time but never understand the overall plan.

Develop a financial budget

With this in mind, you and each ministry leader begin developing a real (not fanciful) dollars and cents budget for your ministry plans. List the materials you will need in order to meet each objective. For instance, if you choose the goal of making church more child-friendly, you probably have made children's bulletins one of your objectives. To fulfill this objective, choose a resource that provides photocopiable children's bulletins. So you have two line items for the budget:

Children's bulletin resource book

Photocopying at 6 cents x n x 52 = cost for one year

(n=the number of children ages 4-10)

Now check out the actual costs of supplies. The Adventist Book Center can recommend a children's bulletin resource and give you the cost to list in your budget. A sample budget form is provided in the appendix.

When the budget form is completed, review it with the church board. It becomes the basis for funding Children's Ministries.

Seek funding

Several sources of funds are open to you: the church budget, donations, and special funds. The funds for the photocopying of a children's bulletin might come from the church office's photocopying or operating budget, or a family or families in the church might donate the money. If all else fails, approach a church or community business that would be interested in either photocopying the bulletins for you or donating the cost. Add to each bulletin a note of acknowledgment naming the business. Wherever the funding comes from, you still need to estimate the cost for your budget, but indicate the source of the funding.

"When making a budget, always ask for more money than you need. You will look good when you come in under budget."

—Ed Manspeaker

When an itemized budget of actual costs is complete, you are ready to begin sharing your plan with the church. Circulate descriptions of the new ministries and itemize materials and funds you need. Church members will very likely purchase some of the materials for you and make donations toward the rest. Keep talking, keep dreaming, keep praying, and keep moving ahead.

Step 4: Publicize Your Ministry

Make as many people as possible aware of your ministry and of ways they can be partners with you: prayer partners, working partners, full partners, occasional partners, or just plain friends of your ministry. The more people you involve, the more aware they and everyone else will be, and the more help you will get.

Keep the congregation aware of what is going on. They will be proud of your ministry and may find additional ways to help.

Keep families informed

You especially need to make sure that community and church families are kept informed of the ministries available. If your beginner Sabbath School has started a great new program of learning centers that begin on time, be sure to report this in the church newsletter. Families who come late or are inactive might be motivated to make extra effort to come on time if they know what their child might be missing. Why not send your story and a photograph to the union paper as well as the local newspaper. They may not always publish your contributions, but you never know when they will. And who knows, a family might be led to attend or even join your church because of the story.

If you do everything yourself, by the way, you will be left carrying the whole bundle. Sure, things will be done your way, but you will not accomplish as much as a team could, and you might burn out trying."

—Noelene Johnsson

Get help with publicity

If you are too busy to write stories, ask the church Communication Secretary to write the stories for you. Be aware that writers do not always see the need to tell your story. You will need to explain why you want a story, what is unique about your story, and what are the key successes you have experienced in relationship to the story. You might even make friends with a reporter at the newspaper who will write the story.

"Remember, we serve a God of abundance."
—Shelby Andress, Search Institute

Step 5: Work Your Plan

Can you think of anything more discouraging to a person whose expectations have been raised by your ministry plan if, after a few months or a year, nothing happens? The person who replaces you in ministry will fight an uphill battle. He will not be able to get support for your plan or for one of his own. Keep the following do's and don'ts in mind:

- Don't present any plan unless you are prepared to work it.
- Don't introduce another plan until you have worked this one.
- Stick faithfully to the plan unless you have a committee vote to modify it.
- Keep the plan practical and doable from the start. You can expand a plan when you have achieved the initial level, but you will lose faith if you shrink it appreciably.
- Implement the plan in stages.
- Begin with something you can implement quickly.

Generate news about your plan

Having a plan, or revisiting the plan is not really news; news is accomplishing something for children. Every time the children are involved in something new, or every time a new part of the plan is put into operation report it in a news story for publication or as a news item in the church bulletin.

Report results

Keep track of the results of each ministry; record the attendance, the number of volunteers and the number of volunteer hours, donated funding, and the program resource you followed or created. At the end of each year report the cumulative figures since the beginning of the ministry plan. Keep interim reports before the church board to let them know what is happening.

Continually evaluate the ministry of your staff

Provide additional training. Take them to conference training events and keep everyone on a path toward certification. Also keep the staff affirmed and fulfilled in their ministry. Evaluate how well you are doing at empowering them. This can be the most long-lasting influence of your ministry because they in turn will empower others.

Evaluate, renew, or redesign the plan

No plan should be open-ended, continuing year after year. On the other hand, every successful plan or program deserves to be repeated. So continually evaluate progress and know when it is time to develop the next 2-3 year plan.

Step 6: Plan for Succession

Anyone who works in Children's Ministries has probably already discovered the high turnover in staff. Leaders tend to migrate through the age levels with their children. Sometimes successful teachers are invited to head other ministries for the church. So it makes sense to plan for succession—somebody to follow you and to keep the ministry growing.

"Normally, the only thing you can be fairly sure of when you leave is that your successor will not be named by you, nor will they perpetuate any trace of you. This is particularly true if you have done everything yourself and had everything your way."

—Noelene Johnsson

However, if your plan is a shared vision to start with, if you have empowered people to follow the plan, and God has guided your ministry, you need not worry about succession. The Lord will provide what is needed. He will provide leaders to build on your ministry. Even though a new broom may sweep clean behind you, sooner or later the seeds you have sown will sprout—the ministries will go on blooming.

Organization

One of the finest gifts you can bequeath to your successor is an organized ministry. Do not organize only the plans, organize and conserve the resources.

- **Organize divisions.** In each division teachers know what to do; children and parents are satisfied.
- **Organize resources.** To organize resources you need adequate locked storage with shelves organized and inventoried. Program guides, copies of successful programs developed and used at your church, and instructions for ordering quarterly materials should be kept on file in each division.

The following are felpful in large churches.
- **Having a central supply area.** A library of teacher resources, including training videos and program resource books, is essential (Resource materials are listed in the Children's Ministries Catalog, and the Quarterly Materials List, both available free from AdventSource). All felt sets, reproducible activity books, resource books, decorations, props, etc., are kept in one area, under the control of an organized person. This prevents duplication, fosters organization, and aids in keeping budgets in line. With an inventory list in hand, it also makes replacement after a natural disaster much easier.
- **Update Visual Aids.** Keep the central supply current. Remove outdated or soiled/damaged visual aids.
- **Organize records.** Names and phone numbers of teachers and substitute teachers, lists of staff birthdays; records on each child kept centrally so that photocopies can go to the next division at promotion time; community lists available for church mailing of upcoming events; a file of your annual budgets; records of your committee meetings; and a copy of your master plan.

Resources

Cionca, John R. *The Trouble-Shooting Guide to Christian Education.* Accent Publications, Inc.

Roehlkepartain, Jolene, editor. *Children's Ministry That Works.* Group Publishing, 1996.

9 Children's Ministries Programs

You and your ministry team have committed yourselves to organizing Children's Ministries in your local church or school. What ministries should be offered? Well-known activities such as Pathfinders or Vacation Bible School come to mind, but there are many more ministry choices! A wise coordinator will begin by strengthening existing ministries, only adding new ones as volunteer help and funds are available.

"Offering more program(s) than you can staff will hurt the overall quality of (Children's Ministries). It is best when one new program is begun at a time."

—John R. Cionca

The following is a list of specific ministries for children with a short description of each.

Adventurer Club
Purpose: The church and the family working together for the spiritual, emotional, and social growth of the child.
Description: A club for families with children in grades 1-4 that sponsors spiritual learning in a social setting. The club usually meets twice a month for 60-90 minutes. Adventurers is a pre-Pathfinder ministry.

Unique features: Children earn awards for completed activities. The program involves parents who network together in a setting that is mutually beneficial to both parents and children.
Resources: Advent*Source* offers a full range of Adventurer resources.

Baptismal Class

Purpose: To prepare children who have expressed a desire to be baptized.
Description: The class studies basic beliefs of Christianity and Seventh-day Adventists so that children understand their relationship and responsibilities to God and to the community of believers. Pastors, teachers, and parents can help prepare children for baptism.
Unique features: Children's baptismal lessons are presented in a concrete form that can be understood at a child's developmental level, rather than using the more abstract, reasoned approach used for youth. Children can take as long as they need in preparation for baptism.
Resources: "It's My Choice" Baptismal Guides by Steve Case (Review & Herald); new baptismal lessons for children ages 8-10 will be available from Advent*Source* in 1997.

Children's Bulletins

Purpose: To provide a child-friendly, spiritual activity for children to do in church.
Description: A two-sided sheet, folded, with word activities, puzzles and pictures for children to complete in church. The bulletin is geared to the same topic as the pastor's sermon. A specific person needs to be appointed to develop, photocopy, and distribute the bulletin insert.
Unique features: Activities for both readers and non-readers can be provided.
Resources: Children's Bulletin Idea Book by Faye Fredericks (Baker). Full-page, reproducible sheets with coloring, dot-to-dot, puzzles and mazes are appropriate for both pre-school and early elementary age levels. Seasonal material is included. Also contact: Communication Resources, Inc., 4150 Belden Village Street - 4th Floor, Canton, Ohio 44718. You can subscribe to their quarterly

children's bulletin service for children ages 3-6 and 7-12. You will receive reproducible bulletins each quarter for both age groups.

Children's Campmeeting

Purpose: Spiritual evangelism and nurture in a camp setting.
Description: Two or three interactive programs a day encouraging the spiritual, physical, social, and mental growth of children, beginners through juniors. Programs are available in a three-year series that includes stewardship, Bible time experiences, and heroes.
Unique features: Offers weekday programming as well as Sabbath programs. The broader time period allows leaders to provide for the physical and social needs as well as the spiritual and mental.
Resources: Stewardship for a Lifetime; Jesus, Then and Now; Follow the Leader. (Advent*Source*)

Children's Choir

Purpose: To give children an experience in expressing worship through music; to train them in singing and in an understanding of music as a ministry outreach.
Description: A musical group just for kids that performs in church. It can be a short-term project in preparation for Christmas, Easter or a complete Christian musicale. Community children can be invited to join the choir and their parents invited to the final performance. Choir devotionals, the music itself, the performance, and the relationships formed can all be a great witness.
Unique features: This ministry brings together church school, public school, and community children. Provides a great opportunity to teach children good music and influence their musical tastes. Offers another window of service to kids.

Children's Church

Purpose: To give children an opportunity to worship in an age-appropriate setting at their own level of understanding, and to take responsibility in worship.
Description: Children's church is a church service just for kids. It begins either when adult church begins or just prior to the sermon.

Children's church is scheduled as often as local need dictates. It is most needed by children ages 2-8, who find it difficult to sit for any length of time.

Junior-age children need their own junior church or to attend the regular service. Children's church is usually generic, with all age-levels worshipping together. It should incorporate all the elements of regular worship such as praise, prayer, sharing, Good News (a mix of local happenings and Scripture), learning from the Word, a children's sermon, and skits that apply the theme to everyday life.

Unique features: Offers children an opportunity to participate and to understand the elements of worship.

Resources: God Loves Me—ages 2-5 (Gospel Light); Living in God's Family—1st - 6th grade (Gospel Light). Kits include weekly programming for a full year with age-appropriate activities and reproducible material. Gospel Light is an interdenominational publisher.

Children's Communion

Purpose: To help children learn about communion and to experience the setting of the very first communion.

Description: A Friday evening program for children and their families. After taking off their shoes, everyone sits on the floor in a setting as close as possible to the Bible description of the first communion. They wash each other's feet, eat the communion bread, and drink the juice. Each part of the service is explained and demonstrated before they take part.

Unique features: Children and their families participate in communion together. It can be like a rite of passage for kids.

Children's Evangelistic Meetings

Purpose: To help children make a commitment to Jesus, and to understand the plan of salvation and the fundamental beliefs of Seventh-day Adventists.

Description: A series of meetings for children that present age-appropriate truths and at the same time the children's parents are attending a public evangelistic meeting. The programs include

Bible stories and doctrine, memory verses, songs, prayers, activities and crafts.
Unique features: Presents a concentrated study of the plan of salvation and the distinctive beliefs as developmentally appropriate.
Resources: Forever Stories Funpack—ages 4-11 (Review and Herald, 1995); My Bible Friends—ages 2-5 by Donna Williams (Florida Conference, 1992): Voyager Teacher's Guide. Ages 4-11 (Advent*Source*).

Children's Lesson/Story in Church

Purpose: To give children the sermon in a nutshell during a time that is uniquely theirs in the church service.
Description: The children's lesson/story uses a verse read from the Bible and an object lesson or story on the subject of the sermon. It takes a total of 5-7 minutes.
Unique features: The children gather up front as children gathered around Jesus. Prepares the children for the sermon to follow. When the pastor tells the story, it reminds the children that he is also their pastor.
Resources: The best stories are told from experience. The Best of Guide; JumpStart!; Nature Quest and Way to Go! Yearly edition of the junior devotional (Review & Herald).

"The stories need to be directed to children ages 2-7, not to the adults in the congregation. Use short sentences and simple words. Try to focus the story to a simple visual."

—Barbara Manspeaker

Children's Prayer Meeting

Purpose: To involve children in the prayer experience and make prayer meeting night attractive to families.
Description: A devotional talk based on scripture that helps to strengthen the children's belief in and understanding of prayer. It includes songs, prayers, and a related craft. Works best if children can meet in a home instead of the church.
Unique features: Offers a special opportunity for family fellowship and spiritual growth.
Resources: Forever Stories Funpack (Review and Herald); chil-

dren's devotional books; Week of Prayer children's devotionals (Adventist Review); VBS lessons make great prayer meeting devotionals. Also "52 Ways to Teach Children to Pray" (Rainbow Books).

Children's Tithing

Purpose: To give children an understanding, motivation, and experience of financial stewardship that is appropriate to their developmental level.

Description: A children's tithe envelope is incorporated into the giving system of the church. Children receive the envelope in Sabbath School when the system is first introduced and parents are given a supply for home use. The tithe envelope serves as a receipt and is returned to the children personally.

Unique features: Implants the habit of systematic giving while the children are still young. Encourages the planning of contributions to the church in advance.

Resources: Children's tithe envelopes are provided by some conferences or can be ordered from Advent*Source* or your Adventist Book Center.

Church Nursery

Purpose: To provide child care during the worship service.

Description: A special room or Sabbath School room is equipped with some Sabbath toys and the materials needed for a simple learning situation. The children do simple activities together in a worship setting and then play with the materials. Parental involvement is crucial to ensure against situations of neglect or abuse. Deaconesses of the church act to coordinate nursery supervision.

Unique features: Offers young parents a quiet time to listen and grow spiritually. Involves teens in service as helpers in the nursery.

Resources: Babies and Toddlers at Church, a complete program for children from birth to two years of age. Weekly lesson plans with monthly theme, songs and activities to help adults communicate Bible promises. (Gospel Light).

Eager Beaver

Purpose: A structured Christian playgroup for children.
Description: The children work on age-appropriate activities to fulfill requirements. Can be useful to stay-at-home moms looking for resources and programs for preschoolers. Great for families to work on together.
Unique features: Children receive "chips" when requirements are completed and parents get a ready-made curriculum for preschoolers.
Resources: A complete set of materials is available from Advent*Source*.

Junior/Earliteen Heritage Tour

Purpose: To help children get in touch with the roots of their church.
Description: The junior/earliteen Sabbath School children and their parents do a tour of Adventist sites.
Unique features: A church or churches can subsidize a tour and it could also be organized through the conference or union. By leading the tour, a pastor can reinforce his relationship with the children and their families.
Resources: Heritage videos by James Nix, suggestions for tours, and books about places to see are available through the E.G. White Estate at 301-680-6550.

Junior Mentoring

Purpose: To give juniors a "hands-on" experience of church community and service.
Description: Juniors are paired up with a mentor who holds a church office. The child will shadow the individual to learn about and help perform their duties.
Unique features: Enables kids to get involved in church work and to make friends with adults.
Resources: Youth Apprenticeship Packet (Advent*Source*).

Neighborhood Bible Camp

Purpose: To reach out into communities and introduce children to God.
Description: A 60-90 minute program of Bible stories, songs, games

and crafts that can be conducted in a carport, family room, front lawn or city park. A neighborhood family agrees to host the Bible camp and invite the children, while the teens of the church run the program and give out snacks.
Unique features: An ideal program for summer interns which involves church members and teens alike.
Resources: A Neighborhood Bible Camp Planbook is available from Advent*Source*. Uses VBS programs and resources. The teens usually have lots of ideas for games.

Neighborhood Bible Club

Purpose: To continue friendships begun at Vacation Bible School.
Description: A 60-90 minute program of Bible stories, songs, games and crafts that can be conducted in a carport, family room, front lawn or city park. A neighborhood family agrees to host the Bible camp and invite the children.
Unique features: This is a family outreach program for children you took to VBS. Invite them to your house for the club and encourage them to bring other community children who can attend VBS next year.
Resources: Forever Stories Funpack (Review & Herald); My Bible Friends by Donna Williams (Florida Conference); Sabbath School materials.

Pathfinder Club

Purpose: To involve kids in discovering their own resourcefulness in nature and the outdoors and to provide an active social climate for kids to make friends with God and each other.
Description: A club for children in grades 5-8. Pathfinders is usually serviced from the youth department of the conference and provides an important ministry to children.
Unique features: Involves kids in practical, outdoors-type learning and service activities.
Resources: Advent*Source* provides a free Pathfinder Leadership Resources Catalog and a complete line of Pathfinder items.

Sabbath School

Purpose: To provide goal-oriented spiritual education that helps kids build a relationship with Jesus Christ, get involved in studying and memorizing scripture, promote the community of all believers and become responsible for service and mission.

Description: A 60-90 minute Sabbath program that is the main focus of a congregation's ministry to children. Programs for children are geared to their age level and are based on a weekly lesson study.

Unique features: The only ministry that reaches all Adventist children. Provides a great opportunity to relate Bible truth to everyday living.

Resources: Children's Ministries Resources for Your Local Church and a quarterly Sabbath School Materials List is provided free from Advent*Source*. Sabbath School lessons, programs, and auxiliary products for the church are published by Review and Herald, Pacific Press, and Advent*Source*.

Summer Day Camp

Purpose: To involve kids in a relaxed summer camp program with a strong Christian emphasis.

Description: A reliable, daily Christian program to keep kids happily challenged in a variety of physical, spiritual and creative activities and coordinated by an adult who is responsible for the program. The day-to-day leadership is provided by college religion and education majors who earn a stipend paid by the parents for tuition.

Unique features: Provides a service for working parents during the summer months. Money from the tuition can enable you to subsidize special Children's Ministries programs.

Summer Ministries Interns

Purpose: To provide help and leadership for special summer ministries programs in the local church.

Description: A program whereby a summer ministries intern is hired by the local church who is responsible for their scholarship money, training, board and supervision. Interns conduct a variety of ministries. Arrangements are made with the conference youth

department for the student to join their week of summer camp training. The intern is accountable to the pastor. The student is not left to manage the youth alone. The program can be run at church where the pastor and/or church secretary are available as needed.
Unique features: Kids respond extremely well to college students. Helps young adults finance their education and gives them the opportunity to make a valuable contribution to the church.
Resources: The local conference youth director; catalogs from Health Connections, Group Publishing or Youth Specialties.

Teen Volunteers

Purpose: To involve teens in ministry to children and to increase the number of volunteer staff available.
Description: Trained teen volunteers assist in the various programs of the church as teachers, musicians and helpers.
Unique features: Teens bring amazing enthusiasm and energy to Children's Ministries. They also provide role models children can identify with.
Resources: Kids Taking Charge: Youth-Led Youth Ministry by Thom and Joani Schultz (Group Publishing, 1995). *The Peer Helper's Pocetbook*, Joan Sturkie and Valerie Gibson (Order from Health Connection Catalog).

Vacation Bible School

Purpose: To reach out to children in the community and lead them to a relationship with Jesus.
Description: Vacation Bible School (VBS) is the church's most popular community outreach program. It involves 5-10 days of 2-3 hour programs, usually held in the summer. With teen help the program can be offered mornings from 9:00 to 12:00, when it is most popular with kids and their families, or in the evenings from 6:00 to 8:30 depending on the community. The program involves a general session, Bible lessons, crafts, and games.
Unique features: Designed as an outreach program for community children; the children of the church learn friendship and witness-

ing skills.
Resources: Three complete VBS kits are available through the Adventist Book Center or Advent*Source*: EarthMaker Mysteries, Friends Forever, and Jesus' Kids in the Kitchen.

Vacation Bible School Follow-up
Purpose: To continue the friendships made at Vacation Bible School.
Description: Parties, special kid events, neighborhood Bible clubs, and other types of personal contacts throughout the year. One-day, holiday events using a VBS format with the addition of seasonal features.
Unique features: The party atmosphere gives a special quality to VBS follow-up events and constant contacts make friends for the church.
Resources: Use VBS lessons and materials.

Try This...
Invite your team to a Children's Ministries "smorgasbord" and treat them to colorful cards which outline the various ministry choices. Ask them to help prepare a "menu" of ministries to offer your local children. Then enjoy a real potluck together!

Children's Ministries Job Descriptions
Children's Ministries Coordinator
The Children's Ministries coordinator brings together all the various ministries for children that a church offers. The coordinator helps leaders plan a calendar for the year that reduces conflicting appointments between the ministries. They act as an advocate for children on the church board and the Sabbath School council, plan a budget and work out funding for the various Children's

Ministries. They help the church plan ministries beyond Sabbath School and look out for the special needs of children in the community, making the congregation aware of how they can help.

Children's Choir Director

The children's choir director may or may not be appointed by the church. They may volunteer for the post and provide a schedule of practices and performances. Generally choir practice begins with a short devotional and a time of prayer. Time should also be made for teaching the children a little about reading music. Children's musicals with pre-recorded accompaniments may be used as well as traditional and contemporary children's church music.

Prayer Partners Organizer

One of the most important tasks a volunteer can accomplish for Children's Ministries in the church is to organize prayer partners as support for those in leadership. To get the prayer partner program underway, the organizer can:
- Send a form letter asking leaders to sign up if they would like to be assigned a prayer partner
- Match volunteers willing to support a person by prayer
- Check periodically for stories of answered prayer
- Organize an annual banquet celebrating prayer partners
- Invite a special guest to speak about prayer

Sabbath School Division Leader

Division leaders are moving more toward a combination leader/teacher role in today's Sabbath School. Because everything that is done in Sabbath School relates to the same objective, the lesson becomes a part of the program. The leader and the assistants plan for the entire Sabbath School hour, sharing responsibilities in the following ways:
- The leader and assistants take turns leading out, using a similar program format to ensure continuity from week to week.
- The leader and assistants have assigned responsibilities, so that

each contributes to Sabbath School and nobody is overloaded. For instance, one person may be responsible for the readiness activities, another for telling the lesson story and reviewing it, and another for singing, prayer, and mission. Every Sabbath one leader has off, in rotation.

The leader is responsible for the division budget, purchase of materials, and staffing, including teen mentors.

Assistant Sabbath School Leader

The assistant stands by to help out in the program as arranged by the leader. Assistants automatically welcome and affirm children. They assist the leader in encouraging teens to help by allowing them to take the assistant's place and training them to do it effectively.

Vacation Bible School Director

The VBS director plans for the overall needs of the staff and organizes the time (the program) and the space (assigns rooms). The director is a behind-the scenes organizer and may also be the up-front leader. The director contacts the conference Children's Ministries department for conference supplementary materials, training and possible financial support.

Vacation Bible School Leader

This person delegates responsibilities for specific tasks, such as music and drama and ensures that children and their parents feel welcome and comfortable in the church surroundings. The leader is responsible for:
- Welcoming the children to VBS each day
- Planning and coordinating the general sessions
- Planning and coordinating the closing VBS program

The closing program will recap for parents what a typical VBS day was like.

Vacation Bible School Division Leaders

Typically, VBS divides into age levels similar to those in

Sabbath School for Bible learning time. The divisions are:

Beginner	(ages 3-4)
Kindergarten	(ages 5-6)
Primary	(ages 7-9)
Junior	(ages 10-12)
Earliteen	(ages 13-14)

Division leader's duties include:
- Take responsibility for the children in the assigned age-level division
- Recruit class teacher/counselors (TCs) to help children do the activities and assist with Bible learning time
- Train class TCs to keep attendance, record and call children who miss a day
- Divide the kids into classes
- Teach songs related to the Bible lesson (which may also be used during the closing program)
- Coordinate the lesson activities, materials and room decorations for Bible learning time
- Tell the Bible stories

For other VBS job descriptions, refer to the VBS Program Guide.

Children's Church Director

A children's church director organizes Children's Ministry teams responsible for the various segments of children's church such as music, prayer, skits, puppets, object lessons, worship theme, etc. The director presides at staff meetings and helps to develop the overall vision for children's church. They may also serve as the leader of a children's church team responsible for the weekly/monthly service. The director's responsibilities include administration, organization, communication and motivation.

The primary focus of the director is to provide creative, new ideas for children's services in a caring, supportive environment.

Pathfinder Director

Pathfinder directors are Master Guides or mature persons who have completed the Pathfinder Staff Training Course. They must be able to work well with the staff and assist counselors and teachers with any problems that may arise.

The Pathfinder director maintains a liaison with the church pastor, youth pastor, and church board. They preside at the club staff meetings and supervise the activities of the club. The director leads out in planning the total program for the year and produces a calendar of events in consultation with the local Children's Ministry coordinator. They also stay in touch with the Pathfinder leader at the conference office and return reports as required.

Adventurer Club Director

The director is responsible for planning and presiding at Adventurer staff and club meetings. They maintain contact with the conference Adventurer director and send in reports as needed. A director should be a person who understands young children, works well with a staff, carries responsibility, possesses an eagerness to recognize new ideas, and shows initiative in implementing those ideas. The Adventurer director also consults with the local Children's Ministry coordinator in scheduling events.

Resources

Adventurer Manual. NAD Church Ministries, Advent*Source*, 1993.
Catalog: Children's Ministries Resources for Your Local Church.
    Advent*Source*, 1996.
EarthMaker Mysteries VBS Starter Kit. Review & Herald, 1994.
Forever Friends VBS Starter Kit. Review & Herald, 1995.
Jesus' Kids in the Kitchen VBS Starter Kit. Review & Herald, 1996.
Pathfinder Staff Manual. NAD Church Ministries, Advent*Source*,
    1990.

10 Understanding Children with Special Needs

Some years ago I was invited to speak to a group of lively primaries. After my talk, I stayed with the children and enjoyed the way they were exploring, interacting and actively involved in their learning experience. Except for one little girl...

After watching her for some time, I discovered she was blind. While the rest of the group took part in various activities and enjoyed the prepared visual aids, she sat quietly in her own little world.

Not once was she encouraged to become involved. Not once was she asked to touch one of the felt figures or place it on the flannel board. Not once was she allowed or encouraged to touch one of the visual aids to help her "see" its size and shape. Not once was the scene on the flannel board described to her, to help her create a mental picture of the life and time of the Bible story—how the houses looked, how the people dressed, etc.

She had lost one of her senses, but had she been encouraged and allowed to learn through the four healthy senses she had left? Had the program been adapted to her needs as well as to the needs of her peers, she could have been as actively involved in the learning as they, and enjoyed every minute of it. Would she be happy in your Sabbath School?

— Birthe Kendall

In the past 10 years child abuse and neglect have risen alarmingly—3.1 million reported cases in the United States during 1994, double the number reported in 1984. Those who would minister to children need to understand the special needs of abused children. But abuse is just one of many problems afflicting today's children.

Special problems that affect children can include:
- Physical disabilities
- Visual impairment
- Hearing impairment
- Learning disabilities
- Emotional disorders
- Mental retardation
- Abuse - physical, mental or sexual

Today's children must cope with the loss of family members through death or divorce, the trauma of natural catastrophes such as tornadoes, bombings, etc., and the day-to-day reality of living in a single-parent home.

Becoming Advocates for Children with Special Needs

The Bible makes it clear that Christians have a duty toward children, especially those with special needs:

"Speak up for those who cannot speak for themselves, for the rights of all."
(Proverbs 31:8)

The habit of overlooking persons with disabilities, unfortunately, is harder to overcome than the lack of ramps in our buildings. That's why children with disabilities need advocates who demand that we give attention to our attitudes.

An advocate for children can challenge people to treat persons with impairment or disabilities as:
- Persons in their own right
- Persons with special needs as well as with needs similar to ours
- Persons who need to hear the gospel
- Persons for whom Jesus would have died, if they were the only ones
- A group belonging to the body of Christ

All children need advocates to speak out for them at home and at church, as well as in the media and government. An advocate needs to stay informed about needs, attitudes and statistics.

People First

When talking about someone who is impaired, use "people first" language. Refer to them as "people with" the specific disability. Do not use the name of the disability as a noun that stands for a person, such as "the disabled."

Making Your Ministry Inclusive

Children with a handicap like to be treated as full participating members along with the other children. But teachers must adapt their presentations to fit the special need.

Jim Pierson, founder and director of the Christian Church Foundation for the Handicapped, reminds us that "inclusion is more than a concept. It is a method of teaching a child with disabilities about God's love in the accepting environment of the church."

"Creating a positive environment in the church will help children of all abilities."

—Jim Pierson

Physical Disabilities

Physical disabilities or mobility impairments can result from spinal cord injury, multiple sclerosis, muscular dystrophy, arthritis, cerebral palsy, polio, aging and a variety of disabling conditions. 1.4 million people in the United States use wheelchairs. Others depend on crutches, walkers, braces or canes to gain mobility if they have paralysis, muscle weakness, poor coordination, nerve damage or still joints.

How to Assist Students with Physical Disabilities
- Familiarize yourself with any special equipment, such as wheelchairs or braces.
- Be sure the classroom and building are accessible.
- Train helpers to assist graciously and sensitively with physical tasks beyond the student's capabilities.

When You're with a Person Using a Wheelchair:

- Talk directly to the person, rather than to someone else with them
- If possible, sit so you are eye level with the person
- Push a wheelchair only after asking the person if assistance is needed
- In guiding a wheelchair down an incline, grasp the push handles tightly so the chair does not go too fast
- For more than one step, keep the chair tilted back at all times while descending or ascending
- Learn the location of wheelchair-accessible ramps
- Do not move crutches or wheelchairs without permission of the individual
- Do not lean on the wheelchair—respect the individual's personal space
- Do not act embarrassed by the person's disability or ignore the individual
- Do not talk about being "confined" to a wheelchair—wheels give the person freedom

Blindness/Visual Impairment

Persons with blindness or visual impairment rely on their other senses to perceive the world around them. People who are blind have no vision or only minimal vision (light perception).

Others may have "low vision" or "partial sight." Low vision refers to limited distance vision. People with low vision are able to see items close to them. They use a combination of vision and other senses to learn to read, although they may require special lighting, larger print, magnifiers and special glasses. Visual impairments can result in blurred or hazy vision and loss of peripheral (side) vision.

How to Assist Students with Visual Impairments
- Use clear, uncluttered visual aids
- Give explanations each time an activity changes or movement is necessary
- Familiarize yourself with appropriate sighted guide techniques
- Explain guide dog etiquette to the class
- Contact Christian Record Services at P.O. Box 6097, Lincoln, Nebraska (402-488-0981) for Braille or large-print materials. They also offer a summer camp program for youth who are blind or visually impaired

A visually impaired child will feel more a part of your class if:
- A volunteer sits with him giving a running description
- You obtain raised tape from her school and outline pictures for coloring. She colors between raised lines
- He brings his Braille typewriter and types something for the children
- The children try to learn to read Braille letters

Children Who are Blind or Visually Impaired	
Need...	**Teachers can...**
1. Words along with gestures	Say "as big as a house" instead of gesturing "this big."
2. Pictures	Use three-dimensional objects they can feel. Describe pictures.
3. Person-to-person contact	Teach the children to give their names before speaking in class. Initiate a conversation with the child to let her know you are there.
4. Physical & verbal direction	Take the child by the arm and speak as you guide him.
5. Colors	Describe the feelings of colors—"It is red; it feels hot."

Deafness/Hearing Impairments

The onset of deafness may occur from birth, gradually after months or years of being able to hear or suddenly as a result of an injury or accident. Signs of this "invisible disability" may include:
- Speaking unusually loud or soft
- Accusing others of mumbling
- Inappropriately answering questions
- Withdrawing from social participation

How to Assist Students with Hearing Impairments
- Don't shout!
- If the child lip reads, be sure they have a clear view of your mouth and face
- If the child wears a hearing aid, keep extra batteries on hand and learn to replace them
- Provide a sign language interpreter, if necessary

Children with Severe Hearing Loss	
Are like this...	**Teachers can...**
1. Tend to act fearful	Make the child comfortable.
2. Cannot hear your commands	Touch them on the shoulder or clap to get their attention. Use words and gestures.
3. Read lips to some extent	Face them when speaking; do not cover your mouth. Do not overemphasize lip movement.
4. Are not stupid	Avoid shouting or showing exasperation. Do not pretend to understand. Ask the individual to repeat the message.
5. Are sensitive	Do not act as if they are invisible. If you have a question that involves them, ask them, not the person with them.

Learning Disabilities

Learning disabilities is an umbrella term for many different problems that make learning difficult. Learning disabilities should not be confused with mental retardation.

A learning disability is a disorder in one or more of the basic psychological processes involved in understanding or using language (spoken or written). This disability may affect a student's ability to listen, think, speak, read, write, spell or do mathematical calculation.

Symptoms of a learning disability include uneven test performance, short attention span, poor memory, impulsiveness, low tolerance for frustration, problems with eye-hand coordination and problems in handling day-to-day situations. Low self-esteem and behavioral difficulties are frequently the result.

Children with Learning Disabilities	
Are like this...	Teachers can...
1. Easily get discouraged	Provide encouragement and acceptance.
2. Often have to repeat tasks	Praise them for the things they do correctly. (Every child can be affirmed for *something*.)
3. Have short attention spans & poor memory	Keep directions and instructions simple and direct.
4. Need "total-body" learning	Involve the different senses—listening, touching, seeing. Use Bible learning activities. Team with a reader.
5. Have a low tolerance for frustration	Recognize the individual's difficulty in handling day-to-day situations due to their limitations. Provide help, if necessary. Do not insist they complete all tasks.
6. Cope with low self-esteem; behavioral problems	Provide opportunities for involvement and sharing, ensuring them success.

How to Assist Students with Learning Disabilities
- Provide for needed breaks in concentration
- Don't "lecture" for long periods
- Continually refocus the student's attention
- Use their name or lightly touch them to draw attention to the task at hand
- Reward attentiveness and cooperation
- Use active learning strategies
- Be visually direct

Attention Deficit Disorder (ADD)

Hyperactivity, inattention and perceptual coordination problems may also be associated with learning disabilities but are not examples of the disorder. Because of the prevalence of attention deficit disorder (ADD), the following tips are included in this section.

The Child with Attention Deficit Disorder (ADD)	
Has a problem...	**Teachers...**
1. Sitting still	Plan an active program. Add actions to the songs. Get kids marching around the room and singing. Allow for a less formal setting so he can move around within limits. Have a volunteer sit exclusively with him.
2. Understanding limits	State the limits—tell her how far she can roam when doing an activity. Don't assume her over-reaching of limits to be disobedience.
3. Being impulsive	Use the child's energy! Have him pass out songbooks; ask him to count money; assign him the role of door monitor.
4. Paying attention	Seat her in front of the class. Assign her tasks ahead of time. Compliment her when she is paying attention. Ask an assistant to give special attention to these children.

Try This...

Pray for special grace to minister to the child with ADD. Then plan for an extremely active Sabbath School. Have the children on their feet often. Playing rhythm instruments or clapping and snapping to the music can also make a program active.

Encourage grandparents or earliteens to volunteer once a month to sit beside the ADD child.

Touch the child's shoulders to encourage them to remain seated when they become restless. Or take a "wiggle-break" for all the children to get the fidgets out!

Emotional Disorders

Child development specialist Dr. Kay Kuzma in *To Understand Your Child* says:

"It is important to understand and work with a child's negative emotions (anger, aggression, temper tantrums, jealousy, etc.) in such a way that he doesn't feel guilty or inadequate. Deep, long-standing emotional problems are complex and usually require not only the patience and insight of the parent, but in addition, the specialized therapy and counseling of a child psychologist or psychiatrist."

Is My Student Emotionally Disturbed?

The following behaviors can help you identify the student with emotional problems. "Please note that none of these may be significant alone," says Kuzma. "But when they occur in combinations, you may have a key to a developing emotional problem."

How to Assist Students with Emotional Disorders
- Be loving but firm
- Encourage the student with praise for even the smallest successes and provide opportunities for them to demonstrate areas of competence
- Ask the student's parents to explain the behavioral interventions and discipline plan used at home and school
- Be consistent in your response to the child
- Don't make promises you can't keep

Emotional Disturbance Inventory

Check those symptoms that you have observed over a 3-week period.

___ Extreme nervousness or irritableness

___ Inability to relax or rest

___ Listlessness/excessive daydreaming

___ Excessive inattention and tendency toward distraction

___ Frequent unprovoked crying spells

___ Lack of interest in surroundings or other children

___ Unusual shyness or quietness

___ Lack of laughter or smiles

___ Over anxious about doing what is expected or "right"

___ Frequent hiding or attempting to run away

___ Repeated aggression (in words or in actions such as hitting or biting)

___ Destructiveness

___ Frequent temper tantrums

___ Frequent complaints of physical problems such as stomachaches or headaches

___ Bed-wetting (after a period of dryness)

___ Unusual or unreasonable fears

___ Marked personality/behavior changes

___ Marked drop in grades (for a child in school)

Keep in mind that emotional disturbances, especially in children, are mostly temporary in nature and frequently accompany a change in the family structure or routine. Parental conflict, divorce, excessive criticism of the child, unrealistic expectations, scholastic pressures, neglect, illness or death of a parent can all contribute to negative emotions in children.

Checklist to Combat Negative Emotions
- Give the child the attention and love needed to grow into a healthy, secure individual
- Correct and deal with negative emotions when they are first expressed rather than let them develop into bad habits
- Reassure the child that everyone has negative emotions

- Show the child how to deal with negative emotions constructively
- Provide the child with an emotionally "safe" environment
- Cultivate a relaxed, cheerful atmosphere

Children with Mental Impairment

Mentally impaired children can be observed sitting in beginner and even primary Sabbath School classes. However, they may remain at or below the primary thinking level. With help, they can learn the fundamental truths of salvation and formally join the church through baptism.

How to Assist Students with Mental Impairment
- Routine is important
- Avoid abstract concepts and ideas
- Use repetition and concise one or two-step directions

Children with Mental Impairment	
Tend to…	**Teachers can…**
1. Be concrete thinkers	Use lots of visual aids.
2. Be sensitive to feelings	Tell Bible stories in terms of how the characters felt.
3. Have a short attention span	Make learning active.
4. Have short memories	Use lots of repetition.
5. Need help with prayer and Bible reading	Teach him one simple prayer. Provide picture Bibles.
6. Lack adaptive skills	Provide transitions: "We are going to get up and sing now." or "It is time to sit quietly."

Conventional Wisdom

Communicating Love

When communicating with someone who has mental impairment:
- Do not be condescending
- Use simple sentences
- Make instructions clear and concise
- Talk with the person even though he may not be verbal enough to respond

Try This...

When teaching mentally impaired individuals, use lots of :

- **Motion songs**

- **Snatches** ("little chunks") of song to get everyone's attention. Make the song quick and emphatic. Break into this song anytime you seem to be losing their attention.

- **Affirmation.** Praise kids for even the slightest effort. Hug them around the shoulders or touch their cheek.

- **Instruments** to play while they are singing.

- **Help with transitions.** Snatches or songs can help define the different parts of the service. Make a picture book that shows the different parts of church or communion. Turn the pages for them when the service comes to a transition, like taking the offering or praying.

- **Whisper chants.** Repeat a phrase such as "Jesus is coming!" Begin as a whisper; each time say it louder until they are shouting.

- **"Song-ettes."** These are the musical equivalent of the little disposable pictures kids take home and stick on the refrigerator. "Song-ettes" are snatches of hymn tunes to which you set any words that fit the lesson. They are sung to teach the lesson and then discarded.

- **Picture Bibles** (they look like comics with a Bible cover). Or glue memory verse pictures into a regular Bible.

- **Opportunities to help** in the community of believers. They can be greeters (along with another person, not by themselves), ushers, Bible bearers, candle lighters, choir members, drummers, plant keepers, one of several persons offering prayer.

- **An occasional chance for segregated worship** with others who are mentally impaired.

"The main qualification to look for in a teacher for people with mental impairment is love. Persons too timid to teach an adult class often do extremely well in this ministry."

—Noelene Johnsson

Children Coping with Loss

Whether it is the loss of a favorite pet, separation from a best friend, their parent's divorce or the death of a special grandparent, each child eventually must deal with loss.

Donna J. Habenicht, professor in the School of Education at Andrews University, says "death is unavoidable for even very young children. Concerns and questions about death are a normal part of growing up. Using teachable moments, such as the death of a pet, helps prepare children for more difficult deaths later on."

Adults are often uncomfortable discussing such loss with children. Children are then left to their own imaginations to figure out why animals or people die or how to cope with the loss of a special friend after a move. Dr. Habenicht suggests some loving, practical ways to help your Sabbath School children deal with loss.

How to Assist Students Who Are Coping with Loss
- Deal with the child calmly
- Provide a refuge of stability and calmness
- Be willing to listen as the child is ready
- Respect the child's way of responding
- Show the child that you understand their feelings
- Help the child understand the grieving process
- Let the child participate in the rituals remembering the loved one
- Give thoughtful answers that a child can understand

Children from Single-Parent Homes

More than half the children growing up in the United States today will spend part of their childhood living in a single-parent family.

Children from Single-Parent Homes	
Tend to... 1. Feel they are alone in this experience; they don't share their feelings readily.	**Teachers Can...** Provide opportunities for children in similar situations to share thoughts and feelings; let them know "God is a very present help in trouble." (Ps. 46:1)
2. Worry about "Who will take care of me?" "Where are we going to live?" Will we have enough money now?"	Listen actively and reassure students that they have permission to feel upset. Explain they can count on God.
3. Must deal with new family relationships and strangers becoming family members.	Help the child stay neutral. Avoid comparisons. Emphasize forgiveness to heal wounds.
4. Need to know what the Bible says about trouble and hope.	Can reassure students that there is hope on this earth and in heaven. God will provide comfort to every child in trouble; He is a "Father to the fatherless."

How to Assist Students from Single-Parent Homes

Here are some specific things that you can do to help your students that come from single-parent homes.

- Spend one-on-one time with them
- Give them positive attention
- Know their family background
- Acknowledge their emotions
- Get them in touch with other single-parent kids
- Make appropriate referrals when needed
- Be a big brother/sister to the family
- Provide resources for the parents
- Be a helper, not a rescuer

Ministering to Children Who Have Been Abused

Child abuse has become a major problem in the United States today. There are over 1.5 million cases of child abuse reported annually and 5,000 children die each year in America as a result of abuse by their parents.

Definition

There are eight types of neglect and abuse but the most serious and the easiest to prove are physical and sexual abuse.

Physical abuse - involves physical injury to the child in some manner that was not accidental. Examples are multiple fractures in the long bones, skull fractures, soft tissue injuries and bruises, and subdural hematoma.

Sexual abuse - everything from indecent exposure to full intercourse and rape.

Physical Abuse

What to Look For
- Cuts, welts or swelling
- Burns; cigarette burns or "donut-shaped" burns from immersion in scalding liquids; burns with a pattern such as from an iron
- Fractures
- Scars with a peculiar pattern - looped or rounded
- Bruises
- Bite marks
- Physically abused children will often have successive injuries

Behavioral characteristics
- Sleep difficulties
- Thumb sucking and nail biting
- Fearfulness
- Listlessness and apathy
- Aggression and violence or withdrawal

Sexual Abuse

What to Look For

- Torn or stained underclothing
- Difficulty with bowel or bladder control
- Soreness, bleeding or discharges from a non menstruating girl
- Trauma to breasts, buttocks, lower abdomen, thighs, genitals or rectal area
- Evidences of self-mutilation (cuts, sores, cigarette burns)

Behavioral Characteristics

- Regressive behavior such as thumb sucking or bed wetting
- Refusal to undress under normal circumstances (getting ready for bed)

How to Respond to a Child's Report of Abuse

Carol Cannon, clinical director and therapist at The Bridge, a Christian center for treating dependency disorders in Bowling Green, Kentucky, outlines these steps for reporting alleged abuse:

- Remain calm or the child may decide not to disclose information in order to spare your feelings
- Allow the child to talk without applying pressure
- Assure the child that reporting the abuse was the right thing to do
- Believe the child—neither the abuse nor the aftermath is their fault.
- Tell the child you will try to help the offender
- Do not, under any circumstances, attempt to verify the child's story or to disprove it
- Don't investigate the matter, confront the perpetrator, or try to determine guilt
- Report the abuse to Child Protective Services
- For the child's sake, do not discuss the matter with anyone but the authorities
- If it is confirmed that abuse has occurred, don't hesitate to prosecute the perpetrator
- Don't explain or excuse the abuser's behavior to the child
- Help the parents of an abused child find a trusted confidant

- Avoiding physical contact
- Poor personal hygiene
- Obsessively good behavior
- Frequent unprovoked anger, such as mutilation of toys
- Panicking or flinching when being touched, like when being tucked in at bedtime
- Continually falling asleep during the day
- Seductive behavior
- Fire setting
- Cruelty to smaller children and animals
- Obsession with punctuality
- Frequent sore throats, difficulty swallowing or choking
- Sudden weight gain or extreme weight loss

Resources

A Guide to Feeling Comfortable with Persons Who Have Disabilities. Bethesda Lutheran Homes and Services, Inc. Watertown, Wisconsin.

Cannon, Carol. "Why the Silence? What You Can Do." *Kid's Stuff,* Spring 1994, pp.6-7.

"Children and Families in Crisis." Children's Defense Fund Report, pp. 68-70.

Dealing with Child Abuse - Video available from AdventSource.

"Dealing with Child Abuse - What to Look For." Kid's Stuff, undated first issue published by North American Division, pp. 10-11.

Doran, Sandra. "What to Do with Tough Kids in Sabbath School! Attention Deficit Disorder." Kid's Stuff, January - March, 1995, pp. 8-9.

Explaining Death & Divorce to Your Kids - Video from AdventSource.

Habenicht, Donna. "Helping Children Cope with Death." Kid's Stuff, April - June, 1996. pp.4-5.

Kendall, Birthe. "Would She Be Happy in Your Sabbath School?"

Kuzma, Kay. *To Understand Your Child.* Parent Scene. Redlands, California, 1985.

Meier, Paul, Donald E. Ratcliff & Frederick L. Rowe.*Child-rearing and Personality Development.* Baker Books, 1993.

Ministering to Children from Broken Homes - Video from Advent*Source*.

Pierson, Jim. *"Including Kids with Disabilities in Your Ministry."* Kid's Stuff, October - December, 1995, pp. 4-5.

Sexually Abused - (catalog #556310) 3-brochure set for parents, victim and church/community. Advent*Source*.

Sprague, Gary. *"Ministering to Single-Parent Kids."* Kid's Stuff, October - December, 1996, pp. 10-11.

Curriculum for Mentally Impaired Youth:

Christian Record Services, P.O. Box 6097, Lincoln, Nebraska (402-488-0981) provide Braille or large-print materials.

Growing Closer to God by CRC Publications.

Hands Uplifted, an audio tape of songs for the Christian classroom by David Morstad, Bethesda Lutheran Homes and Services, Inc. 700 Hoffmann Drive, Watertown, WI 53094. Ph. 800-369-INFO, x418.

Living God's Way by CRC Publications. A mini-course on prayer and worship.

The Friendship Series, Year 1: God, Our Father; Year 2: Jesus, Our Savior; Year 3: Jesus, Our Helper - Teacher's manual, Student resources, Group Leader's Kit. CRC Publications, 2850 Kalamazoo Avenue SE, Grand Rapids, MI 49502-8034. Ph. 1-800-333-8300 within US; 1-800-263-4252 within Canada.

11 Positive Discipline

Discipline, the noun, as used in this chapter, refers to an attitude of self-restraint, orderly and respectful behavior. A teacher who maintains discipline keeps a class of children restrained, orderly and respectful while they are learning.

Styles of Discipline

Authoritarian discipline

Authoritarian discipline lays down rules and polices them. Fear, guilt, and force are used to motivate order and respect. Authoritarian discipline brings instant order to a classroom but does not guarantee self discipline. The adult is in charge.

Permissive discipline

Permissive discipline, on the other hand, appeals to the child's better self and does not enforce obedience. Love and praise are used to motivate productivity. Order, obedience, and self-discipline are not highly valued. The child can take charge.

Authoritative discipline

Authoritative discipline involves the students in decision-making, holding them responsible and accountable. Affirmation and rewards are the chief motivators of order and respect. Students are held to the consequences of negative choices. The adult is ultimately responsible.

Why Discipline Breaks Down

Inconsistent expectations

Problems occur when children learn one type of discipline at home but meet another in the classroom. Either they go crazy with the lack of accustomed restraints, or they rebel against unaccustomed restraint. What is expected of a child away from home is inconsistent with what is expected at home.

Today's child does not learn a common code of manners and rules that govern behavior. The code for families, if it exists, is different for each—even among Christians. As a result, there is bound to be a child or children in each group who seem unable or unwilling to fit in with the accepted values, rules, and conduct of the rest.

Inconsistent teachers

Kids take their cue from the teacher. If a teacher is inconsistent or undisciplined, the students are confused and relax their own self control. Inexperienced teachers add to their problems with class discipline by:
- Beginning the class haphazardly
- Not starting on time
- Not having prepared well for the lesson
- Showing undue familiarity toward students
- Using loud, disrespectful forms of speech
- Joking and teasing excessively
- Failing to model self discipline

Prevention, The Best Cure

The best way to handle discipline, of course, is with prevention. Just as good parents respond to the needs of a newborn baby before it cries, so teachers need to think ahead to meet the needs of students. What are the student's needs? They need to be comfortable, to be mentally challenged, to be actively involved, and to achieve success in learning. Success in learning is gauged in terms of affirmation and approval from both teachers and students.

Children who experience discomfort, boredom, alienation, or failure sooner or later cause problems that disrupt learning and threaten discipline. So it makes sense to care for the child's needs first.

When teachers arrive, they should check the room temperature, air circulation, arrangement of chairs, and the lighting. Early in the week they should already have planned the lesson in terms of student needs—focused activities followed by serious discussions, activities for all styles of learners, materials organized for each activity, and timing that keeps the lesson moving.

Planning for Success

Planning for success is often overlooked when preparing the lesson. A teacher plans for success by deliberately avoiding situations that leave students feeling inadequate, that they failed to know or do or answer as they should. We plan for their success when we make sure students know the answers to questions we ask.

Questions that everyone can answer:
- How do you feel about that? (an activity, the answer to a previous question, a quote, an idea, a situation)
- What do kids your age think about that? (fairness, peace, deceit, violence, or death)
- What are some of the things that kids your age think are unfair? (or cause war, hurt, bad feelings, guilt)

Questions that have more than one possible answer are good, but be prepared to accept any answer. For instance: What is the worst thing about growing old? (Slowing down? Getting deaf? Losing your driver's license?) Any response might be considered correct by somebody someplace.

"A good teacher accepts and affirms all responses and goes on to link them to the concept being taught.

—Debra Brill

A teacher ensures success when asking questions, not about a lesson the students have not yet studied, but about the activities just completed or about shared life experiences.

Earlier chapters in this book discussed differences in learning styles and preferred modes of learning. Learning in their style and mode is a student need. The teacher meets this need by planning activities for all styles and modes.

The traditional lecture style of teaching provides for the needs of some children, but leaves the way open for discipline problems to arise with the others. The traditional teacher can employ tricks of the trade to maintain discipline. The following teaching tips can help prevent discipline problems during stories, devotionals or when it is impossible to provide hands-on learning.

Preventing Disruptions

One cannot prevent all disruptions, but one can avoid many just by recognizing the signals. Keep your eyes roving from one child's eyes to another's as you speak. Read their responses. If they do not return your gaze, they could be bored. Take action. Try one of the following:

- Show visuals and change them as often as the average child's attention span—one minute for each year of their age, plus one. Gestures can help visual learners stay focused.
- Use some unexpected sound effects. Use verbalized sounds that imitate non-verbal sounds. For instance, "Grunt, grunt," "hip-hop," "cock-doodle," "wham," "smack-bang," and "glug-glug-glug," to mention just a few. You might produce some appropriate sounds using a concealed tape recorder or some noise makers. Repetition of cute phrases or rhyming phrases also appeal to the ear of auditory learners.
- Use gestures and body movement as you talk.
- Offer a puzzle or conundrum for kids to figure out or just ask a question. You might say in an exaggerated whisper, "Do you know what happened next?" or "How many do you think he saw?" But don't wait for an answer.

- Tell a story to illustrate your point.
- Introduce an activity—sing an action song or do a brief attention-getter.
- Address a distracted child by name. Insert her name into the story without missing a beat. For example, "A huge brown bear, Daniella, was all crouched ready to pounce on the sheep." Then wait. Daniella's eyes will automatically seek out the person who spoke her name.
- Wait for quiet. Whisper, "I am waiting for everyone to look this way." Don't be afraid to wait. Teachers who talk through disruptions are educating the kids that what you say is not important. Remember, loud commands cause children to get louder.
- Affirm those paying attention. Thank them by name. Soon everyone listens up because they want to please you.

Instant Attention-Getters

When an interruption threatens or kids look bored, before you lose control of the class, switch to one of the following attention-getters.

Song snatches. Sing snatches such as the last line of "My God Is So Good, So Strong and So Mighty." Sing this snatch with a bold beat. Punch the air with your fist on "good" and "mighty." At the end, stamp twice. Song snatches may take only 30 seconds, allowing you to get back to your lesson.

Offer incentives. Award points, stickers, prizes, or time for a favorite game as recognition of improved behavior. But use this type of motivation sparingly and as a last resort. Incentives soon lose their appeal. However, they may be the only thing that works with a difficult child.

Use an interactive style. Tell the kids that every time you say a word, such as "pray," they are to say a given word (such as "amen") or they do an appropriate action such as to make waves when they hear the word "water."

Bubbles of fun. Interrupt the lesson or story by bringing out a bubble maker and sending a stream of bubbles over the group.

The children will jump up and burst them. Say, "Bubbles are God's way of giving out smiles." Challenge the kids to look closely for colors in the bubbles. If the light is right, they may see rainbows reflected on the surface and remind them of God's promise to Noah. After 2-3 minutes put the bubble-maker away and say "Now let's look for God's promises in today's lesson."

Funny face. (For preschoolers.) Say the following verse, pausing for the gestures after each line:

Wiggle your eyebrows,
Wiggle your nose,
Wiggle your eyelash,
Wiggle your toes.
Stretch up tall,
Sway in the breeze,
Sit tall in your chair
As still as can be.

—Adapted

Make up a second verse to say while seated. Replace "wiggle" with "God made." At the end say, "Thank You, God." Then return to the lesson or program.

Happy and you know it. Stand and sing "If You're Happy and You Know It," doing the actions for each verse. If you have room, do another verse, replacing "clap your hands" with "hop about," "touch your toes," and finally, "sit right down."

Yarn spinners. (Juniors) Stop the lesson and give everyone several pieces of yarn. Tell the kids that when you say, "Go," they have exactly 2 minutes to connect their pieces of yarn, so as to spin a long thread. See how long a string they can form. When done, admire the length of their string, collect it up, and return to the lesson.

Balloon float. Launch a balloon and see how long the kids can keep it aloft by blowing. Then haul in the balloon and drift back to the lesson, reminding them that God keeps them afloat as long as they keep depending upon Him.

Emotionally Safe Classrooms

We know students learn best in a classroom that is safe and comfortable. Many Sabbath Schools around the world cannot provide physical comfort, yet kids feel comfortable there and keep coming back. Why? Because the emotional climate is safe and accepting.

Undisciplined behavior threatens the emotional climate for children. They are never sure whether the unruly person will physically or verbally attack them. Teachers need to address behavior problems immediately, objectively, and fairly.

To handle major disruptions quickly and fairly, while maintaining your cool, follow these simple steps:

1. Ask what happened. Don't assume that you know what happened and start assigning punishment. Fairness requires you to listen to both sides. If possible, do this quietly without disrupting the class.

2. Ask why. There may be a perfectly understandable, non-violent reason for the disturbance. Understanding the cause helps everyone to forgive and forget. But if the problem is too big or has occurred often, continue with the next step.

3. State the situation. Ask those most closely involved if they agree with your assessment. If they don't agree, listen while they explain their perception. Restate the situation.

4. Suggest a consequence. Moving the offender to another chair, near a teacher and away from close buddies, often solves problems. A quick, loving consequence that retains as much as possible of the child's self respect helps the classroom climate. Assigning a child to a "time-out" chair can be used as a last resort.

To handle minor disruptions, recover control quickly and without fuss, or move the child quietly but firmly, redirecting the child's attention. Direct lots of love and attention to previous offenders, thus surrounding them with emotional safety. Go out of your way to help them feel successful in the learning situation. Then gradually wean them from constant attention.

Friendly Classrooms

Friendly teachers are the surest way to develop friendly classrooms with a warm, accepting climate. Friendly teachers do lots of the following:
- Genuinely love kids
- Greet students by name, both in and out of the classroom
- Show they are glad to see each person
- Minimize personal difference and behavior problems
- Like talking to kids
- Want to get to know kids
- Are interested in what other people think and say
- Look into the eyes of the person who is talking to them
- Listen with their whole attention when a student speaks to them
- Smile a lot
- Show appreciation for little things
- Perceive everyone else as their friends
- Think the best of others

Students in friendly classrooms relate to each other as friends. Kids usually respect and cooperate with their friends. But the biggest obstacle to friendliness in an Adventist Sabbath School is, unfortunately, our biggest asset—church school. Children from a tight-knit school don't have to exercise their friendship skills at church, they just fall in with the cliques they belong to all week. Cliques can breed disrespectful behavior, challenging teachers and alienating those students not in the clique.

Self-discipline in the Classroom

Having brought the classroom under control and established routine for self-directed activity, the teacher needs to teach self-discipline. This is, after all, the goal of all discipline. How can Children's Ministries contribute to self-discipline when the teacher only sees the child for an hour a week? To answer this question, consider the following points:
- Leaders and teachers must remember that alone they cannot grow self-discipline, but God can.

- The more time a child spends with God, the more chance God has to get through to the child and the more likely growth in self-discipline will occur.
- The time we spend sharing God's love with students helps them relate to God and be open to His prompting toward self-discipline.
- Consider how long it has taken you to learn self-discipline; don't expect more of your students.
- Scripture memorization, daily prayer and Bible study will some day pay off in self-discipline. That's why we encourage habits of daily study.
- God and good teachers both motivate kids toward self-discipline just by loving them.
- Self-discipline is "caught" as much as it is taught. Teachers need to model self restraint and respect for others.
- Teach children to make good choices and to accept the consequences.
- Challenge the students to show they are growing up and can assume responsibility. Treat them as responsible people.

Noise, Reverence, and Learning

Teachers who picture discipline in terms of quiet rows of unmoving children may find it difficult to adjust to the realities of active learning. Active learners work freely in groups, each doing their own activity. When the activities are done, the kids are ready to sit and talk about what they learned.

The teacher, instead of taking the lead role and starring in the learning process, has turned coach. Standing on the sidelines, she encourages the team and affirms their efforts. The students, instead of watching the teacher do everything up front, take learning into their own hands. They follow directions and come up with their own answers.

"People often ask, what do you do about disruptive children. I tell them. 'How about changing the activity. Perhaps cutting and pasting.'"

—Mary Martinez

It is not surprising that in today's classroom the legitimate sounds of learning replace the idealized quiet of yesterday's class. Nobody expects active learners to be quiet, and if they are, we know it won't last long.

The potential for disruption, rebellion, and mayhem exist, but the motivation does not. If the activities are planned ahead, the materials available, and the students are challenged to discover or make something, they are too interested and too busy to deliberately cause trouble. However, just in case a disruptive situation occurs, check out the disruption stoppers below.

Disruption Stoppers for Active Learning

Provide adequate supervision. Each group of 5-6 students needs an adult or teen teacher/counselor (TC). The TC facilitates and rallies the group to carry out the leader's directions. The TC motivates the kids to see how well they can do. The TC does not need to prepare ahead for this role.

Affirm children. Praise children often for both positive behavior and being productive. Affirmed, productive children feel successful and seldom intentionally cause problems.

Encourage independence in learners. Show them where to find supplies; give permission to get them without asking. Develop routines for cleaning up. Teach kids to mop up spills for themselves and each other.

Try out each activity ahead of class. This can avoid nasty surprises in class; they unhinge your self-confidence and disrupt learning.

Provide clear directions. (See chapter 7)

Emergency Measures

In an extreme case when the class is losing control, take action at once. The following strategies may depend on the group and the situation.

- **Stop the lesson or program.** Insist on having everyone's attention and wait until you get it. You may need to flip the lights off for a minute or use some other device to get their attention.

- **Praise**. Thank the students who were quick to respond.
- **Change the activity, giving clear instructions.** You might say, "I am sorry you don't want to see this video. So let's skip it and do (name the activity)." If the students beg to see the video, tell them their cooperation with the next activity will determine whether you show it later.

If the disruption involves only a few students, try moving them. If this has already been tried, take the ringleader outside for a heart-to-heart chat. Ask what the problem is and listen to the concerns. State the behavior changes necessary for reinstatement in the class.

A time-out may be necessary for the ringleader. Time-outs work best with younger students.

Taking Responsibility

Undesirable behavior is the responsibility of the person who exhibited that behavior, but a breakdown in discipline is a leader's responsibility. Lectures about behavior or sending children to their parents are the teacher's confession that:
- He or she has failed
- Preventive measures have not been taken
- Warning signals have gone unheeded

A teacher who prepares will not allow discipline to get to the stage where it breaks down. An ounce of prevention preempts the need for cures.

"Always start with the assumption that students are on your side. Don't let little infractions get blown up into mighty mistakes or unpardonable sins."

High Interest Noise Breakers

- Lower your voice so the kids have to listen harder.
- Raise your hand with your elbow bent, your palm out toward the noisemakers.
- If the kids are laughing loudly at something that has just happened, laugh with them and wait for a lull. Then raise your hand and call for quiet.
- Call for quiet by saying one of the following:
  "Let's listen up."
  "When you are quiet I will explain . . .".
  "Which group will be first to settle down?"
  "Are you ready to hear (whatever)?"
  "As soon as we finish (whatever) we are going to do (whatever)."
  "As Barry was saying . . .".
  "Let's remember where we are."
  "Let's settle down now."
- Announce the next activity. You may even skip what you had planned to do next, knowing that the students need a change of pace.
- Give a prearranged signal, such as one of the following, as appropriate to the age level:
  - Sing a song snatch.
  - Flip the lights off until the kids quiet down.
  - Clap a complicated rhythm that the kids will imitate or complete.
  - Play several chords on the piano.
  - Bang a couple spoons together.
  - Ring an unusual bell or play a music box (a big hit with kids).
  - Say "Hear Ye!" and cup your hands to your ears. Award a point to the first group to cup their hands to their ears and look your way. (Without speaking, make a show of looking all around the room until quiet reigns. Then quickly add a point to the running tally on the board and announce whatever comes next.) At the end of class, let the winning group take a bow.
  - Count to three. (Kids know to be silent and looking your way by "three.")
- Play "King Solomon Says" (a Sabbath version of Simon Says)
- Play "Do This; Do That." (The kids imitate your actions when you say, "Do this," but not for "Do that.")
- Do a chant, punctuated with claps, that the Kids echo.

Questions Teachers Most Often Ask

Q: My class has come alive since I began to use active learning. But the previous teacher keeps coming in and complaining that the class is noisy. I feel like quitting.

A: Noise is not necessarily bad. A lively learning situation naturally generates a comfortable level of noise. Moreover, a completely quiet classroom may be one in which no learning is taking place or where the students are in a stupor. Be sure your class experiences periods of calm and periods of bustle, activity, and yes, maybe noise.

The wise teacher is more concerned with learning than with noise levels. However, others in the church will rightfully be concerned if the noise in one classroom disrupts the learning in another. So encourage students to restrain boisterous outbursts. Usually just a reminder that there is a class next door restores quiet.

Act toward the concerned former teacher with humor and deference. Sound apologetic; thank her for her concern and forget it. Think of her words as drops of water on your feathers; then just flick them off. But please don't quit!

Q: What can I do with a child who constantly disrupts? Rewards don't work with her.

A: Try to find out why the child interrupts. Possibly the child has a physical problem that you cannot cure. Talk to the parents and maybe to the child's school teacher. Ask them if they have observed the problem and if so, how they cope with it.

Draw up a chart, attach it to stiff poster board and attach a pencil on a string. Draw five lines across the page, write the child's name at the top and write "Sabbath—1" on the first line. Talk to the child privately and explain that you will keep the chart under the child's chair. Nobody else will have a special chart; it is your secret. Next week, every time the child interrupts, you will quietly draw an X on the first line.

At the end of class the next week, you and the child count the X's and write the total at the end of the line. Explain that you will do the same the following week, (Write "Sabbath—2" on the next line) and if the number of X's is fewer, he gets a sticker after class. Show an extra special sticker that he will get if the number of X's is fewer than five.

Q: Some of my students constantly talk about TV. I can't get them to think seriously.
A: The next volume of this book will talk about teaching methods. For now, try to motivate the children to have a day without TV. Talk about it a lot for it may take a long time to see any change. Go out of your way to motivate lesson study and memorization of the Bible verse. Offer a big, I mean BIG, prize for being able to say 13 verses on Thirteenth Sabbath. When the day comes, have as many gifts as you can afford. The first children to get done saying their verses are first on the list to get a prize. You may have enough prizes for kids who learned only 5 verses. Have some lesser prizes for the rest who tried. Next quarter, a lot more kids will be studying the lesson and learning the verse.

Q: What can I do about a non-stop talker in my class?
A: Pray about it and then choose one of the following options:
- Hold your hand, palm out, in a "stop" gesture. Say "(Child's name), it's my turn."
- Try the personal chart described under question 2.
- Make up some coupons that say, "Thanks for listening." Give a coupon to any child in the class, at any time you see them listening. Attach envelopes to a bulletin board for each child to keep their coupons in. At the end of the quarter they can redeem coupons for gifts.

Q: Some kids bring GI Joe and other toys to class on Sabbath.
A: Sometimes kids feel alone at church so they bring a toy for company. If you take away the toy, the child may feel as unwanted as the toy is. Provide a place to park toys or provide chairs for toys. Treat dolls as people and help them join in the singing and praying. Kids will soon tire of this and leave them home.

Q: What do I do with kids who hurt others?
A: Children need only a few rules; you can insist on them, stating them often enough so the children memorize them.
- We don't hurt people.
- We don't hurt things.
- We respect God and the Bible.
- We respect our teachers and friends.

When children hurt others, it's time to sit in the time-out chair. But remember, hurting people hurt others. Spend a little extra time with this child. Emphasize how much God loves him. Tell him how God changes people and pray with the child. You might even make a chart as in question 2.

Q: What can I do about kids who always come late?
A: Coming late has two causes—either other people keep the child late, or the child is not motivated to come and keeps the family late. It all boils down to motivation. If your Sabbath School is so exciting that children cannot wait to get there, parents will know and things will probably change. Remember, the big hit with the kids is not the decorations so much as the activities.

Q: What do I do about kids who don't get involved in singing, answering or doing.
A: Don't try to sing at the beginning of the program, but do some activities first. Get the kids doing stuff in small groups and then bring them together for singing and prayer. Be serious about Bible study with activities. Serious fun gets kids loosened up to get involved. If all the kids act this way, invite them to bring some religious music to listen to instead of singing.

As boys voices begin to break, they are reticent to sing. Accept the fact that juniors do not sing loudly. Let them make music with combs and tissue paper or form a puppet choir (the kids make brown bag puppets and then make the sounds for the puppets).

Resources

Crisci, Elizabeth Whitney. *Five-Minute Bible Fun, Lesson Openers.* Shining Star Publications, 1991.

Holt, Pat and Grace Ketterman, M.D. *Choices Are Not Child's Play.* Harold Shaw Publishers, 1990.

Roehlkepartain, Jolene. *Wiggle Tamers.* Group Publishing, 1995.

12 Staffing Children's Ministries

Finding people to staff the programs is one of the biggest problems for leaders of the various Children's Ministries. Not only does it take time to call around, but sometimes the refusals undermine a leader's morale.

Many good books have been written on the subject of recruiting volunteers, and lots of good advice has been given. The conventional wisdom boils down to one simple truth: if you know how to do it, recruiting staff need not be a big deal. The following are some pointers to keep in mind:

- Helpers in Children's Ministries are volunteers; we treat them differently from employees.
- The goal of recruiting is ministry, not staffing: help volunteers match their spiritual gifts with a ministry need.
- Volunteers are more likely to be attracted to ministries that are alive and on the cutting edge.
- People are more likely to commit to a specific, short-term task than to a year in a given ministry.
- The easiest recruiting pool for next year is this year's volunteers.

Laying a Foundation for Volunteer Ministries

People who are pressed into service at the last minute seldom last long in Children's Ministries. Start laying a foundation for volunteer ministries that will outlast you. Begin by securing the spiritual foundation—a front-line of "prayer warriors" and "prayer guards" who have a heart for your ministry. Then nurture and train your volunteers so they will experience empowerment and fulfillment. Look for people whose gifts fit the opportunities in Children's Ministries.

Prayer warriors. People, many or few, who hold up your ministry in prayer even though they may not be actively involved in the ministry are important. Seniors who are slowing down, adults who care but do not have the gift of teaching, or parents who cannot be involved at this time, all make great prayer warriors. They stay in touch with you and pray about the specifics that trouble you. Their greatest contribution is in praying that God will provide the right person to fill each specific staff vacancy. You need to meet with prayer warriors once in a while, reminding them of the high value you place on their intercession. Report often of new recruits and staff replacements to keep this ministry active.

"I usually set up a prayer support group that prays from the first planning session through the end of Vacation Bible School. It certainly makes VBS go smoother; the answers to prayer bolster our spirits."

—Judi Rogers

With a supportive foundation of prayer warriors, recruiting volunteers will take on a whole new dynamic for you. Ideally, the prayer warrior program is developed by the children's coordinator, but in the absence of strong overall leadership, any leader can develop their own prayer warriors.

Nurturing Volunteers

Having laid a spiritual foundation for volunteer ministries, a church needs to actively nurture volunteers. Take care of those who volunteer this year and recruiting will be a breeze next year. Volunteers can be nurtured spiritually through any or all of the following:

Prayer guards. Church members are paired up with volunteers. Prayer guards do for their volunteer what prayer warriors do for you. They hold up the volunteer in prayer and send them encouraging messages. Previous volunteers make great, empathetic prayer guards. This program of partnership in prayer will grow in effectiveness as you give it a high profile in the church. You can do this by holding an annual prayer guard and volunteer celebration dinner. The volunteers can report special blessings from prayer guard support.

Volunteer dedication services. Held each fall (or whenever leadership changes hands at your church), dedication services can remind the congregation of the value the church places on its volunteers. Be sure to include prayer guards in the dedication service.

HIS Ministry. Induct volunteers into HIS (Honor Instead of Salary) ministry. There need not be any organization to HIS Ministry; people just buy into an idea, making it "cool" to volunteer.

Recognition of volunteers. Feature volunteers on Children's Sabbath or recognize them in church at the start or close of a ministry (the Adventurer year, a Pathfinder evangelism project, Vacation Bible School, etc.). Report the total volunteer hours involved in a successful event. Give recognition for all the free time and personal sacrifice involved: get freebies for volunteers such as sponsoring them to training events, get them ABC discounts, offer them choice or discounted tickets to non-church events, etc. You might even ask an adult Sabbath School class to adopt or sponsor a missionary in your children's division. The class prays for, affirms, and writes notes of encouragement to their missionary.

Make their work easy. A church needs to make the volunteer's work as easy as possible. The church office might obtain their supplies, such as paper, pencils, markers, glue, scissors, and photocopies. Set up a system for requesting such supplies and a budget.

Remember their birthdays. Help them feel part of a warm, caring team. This is something the church office might volunteer to do as their way of affirming volunteers.

Most of the above ideas for nurturing volunteers should become standard practice for any and all volunteers in your congregation. But don't wait for others to catch the vision. Launch it yourself at whatever level you work in Children's Ministries.

"We once did a thank you luncheon for all the VBS volunteers. Affirming volunteers ensures that they want to help next time I need them."
—Judi Rogers

Communicating with Volunteers

Volunteers like to belong to a team that accepts them. Team spirit can be fostered by good communications and thorough organization. In other words, everyone needs to know what is going on and how to get things done. Regular teachers' meetings provide opportunities for two-way communications and provide a time when the team can work on matters of organization.

But you need to give volunteers plenty of reasons to come to teachers' meetings. Provide lots of humor, energy, and creative touches as well as worthwhile planning and training. If you go all out, volunteers will hate to miss a meeting. Anytime you meet with your volunteers, do little ice-breakers to help teachers get to know each other better.

Training Volunteers

There are many ways to provide training for volunteers. Choose more than one way that best suits the situation at your church.

- **The big training event.** Take your volunteers to at least one big training event each year. Your conference or a nearby conference

Ice-Breakers for Volunteer Meetings

Ice-breakers are fun activities that get people talking and getting to know each other. Try one of these activities at your next staff meeting.

Music matches. Ask everyone to choose a song that best describes them as a person. They have time to think and choose the song then write it on a card and pin it to their collar. They go around asking, "What's your song?" and listening as people explain themselves in terms of a song. To wrap up, ask several people to report an interesting response they encountered.

Birthday lineup. Ask everyone to lineup against a wall according to their birthdays. Tell them that you are timing them. Then stand back and watch what happens. See who organizes the group. After several minutes, start calling the months of the year in order and see who stands where. Encourage everyone to note the person whose birthday comes right before their own.

Personal trivia who's who. Find out who's who in terms of personal trivia. Give everyone a card on which to write one personal fact that others are not likely to know. Collect the cards and read out the facts. Everyone tries to guess who the fact refers to.

Quirky sit-in. Ask everyone to stand up. They must sit when they hear a statement that is true of them. Sample statements such as "Learned to read before starting kindergarten," "Can play lacrosse," "Was born on February 29," "Has read a book this month," "Has straightened her sock drawer in the last week," "Likes licorice," "Has eaten in an Ethiopian restaurant," "Makes sushi," "Likes lime ice cream," "Likes chocolate," etc. Ask one or two people to tell about their experience with the statement that caused them to sit down.

Use kid's ice-breakers. Use readiness activities from VBS Bible lessons or Junior Teen Plus (the program helps for juniors and earliteens). Ask the junior/earliteen leader to choose an ice-breaker for the group.

may hold fall or spring workshops at a youth camp or at a large church. Don't miss this event.
- **Individual training opportunities.** The Adventist Children's Ministries Association (ACMA) provides great training opportunities, connected to their volunteer certification program.
- **Regularly scheduled meetings.** Use monthly or quarterly staff meetings or an occasional weekend retreat. You might designate a night the first month of a quarter for training. When you involve volunteers in a weekend training event, you may want to provide a change of format for the kids' programs, such as a combined Sabbath School, to make it easier for a stop-gap team to hold the fort.

Reasons to Meet With Volunteers

You need to meet often with your staff in order to provide spiritual, emotional, and practical support for members of your team. We all need the support of others; staff meeting time is a good time to make sure your staff are surviving!

The wise man made a great case for support time when he said:

"Two are better than one, because they have a good return for their work: If one falls down, his friend can help him up. But pity the man who falls and has no one to help him up! Also, if two lie down together, they will keep warm. But how can one keep warm alone? Though one may be overpowered, two can defend themselves. A cord of three strands is not quickly broken."

—(Eccl 4: 9-12, NIV)

More Reasons to Have Regular Staff Meetings

- **Increase effectiveness and satisfaction.** Meetings give volunteers a chance to express their needs and get a boost for their ministry.
- **Improve teacher's skills.** When teachers feel comfortable enough to ask for advice and to admit they need help, they are ready to pick up tips from you and from one another.
- **Help the teachers meet kids' needs.** Teachers can help each other understand the needs of their students as they discuss class situations together.
- **Set the vision.** Staff meetings can keep the church's shared vision before the volunteers. When everyone works toward the same goals, the ministry is sure to meet its goals.
- **Ensure good organization.** Organization soon breaks down if people are not reminded of structures that are in place to help them. The two-way communication of the staff meeting assists overall organization.

Planning Meetings for Volunteers

For volunteer meetings to be successful, you will need to find the best time and place. Locations to consider are your home, a restaurant, the fellowship hall, a park, the beach, etc. You might ask an adult class to prepare the setting and food for your meeting as part of their missionary vision. Advertise the meeting in advance in the church bulletin, in posters, and personal invitations.

To boost attendance, offer door prizes such as candy apples, wrapping paper before Christmas, a certificate stating the church will pay for drinks for the person's whole division or department next Sabbath. Give people many reasons to feel glad they came.

Try some of the following ideas to bring sparkle to staff meetings and to create a team spirit at the same time.

"Quarterly staff meetings allow us to plan our programs in advance. This saves lots of time in the end. It provides a chance to find resources and develop creative ideas."

—Judi Rogers

Plan the meeting around a theme. Make it festive. Cultural themes, such as Spanish night, or African culture night, can provide ideas for keeping ministry multicultural. This is a much needed emphasis, particularly if your church is not multicultural. Seasonal touches are always appreciated. Possible themes and titles for the event might be:
- *Golf:* Tee-time Teacher Enrichment and Education
- *Video:* Molder of Dreams, 90 minutes
- *Mystery:* mystery guest speaker—mystery theme
- *Basic Training*—wear fatigues. Go over the basics of Children's Ministries. Use brown table cloths, ugly balloons, etc.

Make it a training event. At each meeting do two games and a craft. Put directions on card stock so the staff can file them for future use.

"Sometimes I have found it helpful to involve staff volunteers in doing the activities or crafts that the kids would later do."

—Judi Rogers

Make it a social event. Provide socializing with ministry. Help volunteers and their families get to know each other. Have an occasional volunteer potluck on Sabbath.

Basics for Successful Meetings

In order to ensure success, staff meetings need the following to be arranged:

- **Child Care.** Offer payment to offset church school tuition for a couple of reliable eighth or ninth graders.
- **Time Limits.** Clearly state starting and ending times, keep meetings short and hold them regularly (once a month).
- **Advertising.** Use advance publicity and personal contact.
- **Affirmation.** Affirm those who come and don't complain about those who don't. Don't expect 100 percent attendance.
- **An offering.** Collect one to help pay the baby-sitters.

Showing That You Care

Volunteers appreciate a pat on the back—a little affirmation goes a long way. You can affirm volunteers by stopping by a classroom and asking how it's going. Also ask if there's anything they need. Your motto should be: stop, look, listen. Volunteers like you to do all three. Chart your progress so you don't miss anyone or get someone to chart your progress for you.

Other ways to give a pat on the back are:

- Get the senior pastor to send a handwritten note of affirmation once a year.
- Along with the supplies from the church office or the Sabbath School secretary, attach a short note of thanks and/or some candy.

- Collect Sabbath snippets, anecdotes from the leaders and teachers of all Children's Ministries in your congregation. Print them in the church newsletter.
- Take Polaroids of the division and make a scrapbook for the leader.
- Make survival kits for each leader; make it cute and funny. For example, include a bandaid with a note saying, "To patch your nerves before class."
- Keep a list of substitute leaders and teachers you can call in an emergency.
- Have kids make cards for their regular teacher when you know they'll have a substitute.
- Create a teacher bulletin or newsletter.
- Schedule interviews with teachers during the eleven o'clock service so they can share their ministry. Have a pastor or elder do the interviewing. Ask them what the kids are doing that is exciting and how the rest of the church can help.
- Visit the teachers at home. Take kids with you. Say, "Not a trick, but a treat!" Give something like scented candles with a message that matches the theme of affirmation.
- Teacher for a day. Honor someone for one Sabbath. Consult with the leaders to get their nominations. You interrupt Sabbath School to give a large button that reads, "I am teacher for the day," or make the presentation at the church announcements time.
- Decorate their door with a graffiti wall that kids and adults can add to. (Best for longtime teachers.)
- Give plants and flowers.
- Honor the teachers with OREOs (Outstanding Religious Education Ovations); give oreo cookies with the honors.
- Certificates for Subs—"for coming through in a crunch" (give crunch bar).
- On a wall in the Sabbath School wing of the church, affirm teachers with a display, such as: "We're grapeful for you"—show a bunch of grapes with volunteer's names on the grapes.
- Give members of the congregation valentines to write for teachers.

- Along with the leader's copy of *Kid's Stuff* magazine, attach a tea bag or bubble bath with a note that reads, "You deserve a break today."
- Singing telegrams—take a group of kids to sing to teachers and present them with a small gift.

Recruiting Volunteers

Gender Inclusiveness

Children's Ministries are enriched when men volunteer as leaders, teachers and helpers. Children love to hear men tell stories, relate true-life adventures, and tell how they came to know Jesus. Here are some suggestions for getting men on your Children's Ministries team!

"It's hard for men to want to get involved when they see only women working with children in the congregation."

—Darrell Fraley

But once you turn that percentage around and 20 percent of your volunteers are men, other men will find it easier to join.

Some prefer to get involved in small steps. A man might agree to help kids find their way back to their rooms from the bathroom instead of teaching a class. A teen might like to interact with kids at a learning center. Seniors might provide healthful refreshments. Gradually their involvement may increase. Any effort, no matter how small, is significant if it contributes to the overall goals of Children's Ministries.

Follow a strategy.
- Mention a particular talent or skill the person possesses—be specific.
- Call and ask them to help with a specific task relating to their talent or skill.
- Never approach anyone to do Children's Ministries while they are standing with a group of peers! They may be embarrassed and refuse an assignment they might otherwise have accepted.

- Let volunteers do it "their way." People can be unique and creative in their approach to activities and lessons.
- Get curriculum resources that anyone can use. Try science experiments, nature talks and lots of experiential learning activities.
- Get Children's Ministries well organized. Being well organized shows volunteers the importance of this work. Use ministry/job descriptions, mission statements, lists of goals, flow charts, etc.
- Resolve all major personality conflicts. People are attracted to a ministry where volunteers empower and support each other.
- Maintain cleanliness and order. Some people don't get involved in decorating rooms, but they do like the environment to be organized and pleasant. Many will base their decision to join on how they feel about the learning environment.
- Use a team approach to ministry. Make it clear that a team-teaching approach is valued. Rotating leaders and teachers takes the strain out of "always being up front" and makes it more interesting for the students.
- Show the results of Children's Ministries. Many judge work by its productivity. They like to be part of a successful ministry—they want to see results! Tell what the Lord is doing in your class and what is exciting about working in Children's Ministries. In older classes, you can work out a strategy for inviting and preparing children for baptism. Affirm teachers and leaders for their role in leading the candidates to Jesus.

Strategy for Recruiting

One strategy that worked well for veteran junior leader, Jerry Bartram, is worth trying.

With all the great ideas and activities you employ in your ministry, parents are going to hear about it and stop by to watch. Before they leave, ask: "What is something neat that God is doing in your life?" If the person seems to have an active spiritual life, invite them to attend your staff potluck. At the potluck, staff members can share the excitement and fulfillment they find in this ministry. Then invite the newcomer to join. If possible, invite couples to experience ministry together. Later the kids can follow up by calling or stopping by to encourage the couple to join the ministry.

Other tips for recruiting.

- Pray about filling vacancies. Begin praying and planning long before the need actually arises.
- Don't lay a guilt trip—("You owe me one!")
- Don't appeal on the basis of helping you out in a pinch.
- Tell them what strengths you see them bringing to the ministry.
- Tell the spiritual blessings you get out of the ministry.
- Don't ask for an immediate response. Ask them to pray about it.
- Don't ask as they are leaving church; call on them at home.
- Follow up with a phone call.
- Don't take "no" for an all-time answer. If you get an initial turn down, don't assume they will never be willing to volunteer. Ask them again—using some of the suggestions given.
- Ask the senior pastor to make a follow-up phone call, giving ministry reasons for the person to get involved.

"Kermit, have you noticed something?" the children's division leader asked innocently. "We need to involve more men in the cradle roll division!"

"You're right," I agreed, "some children could grow to be 15 years old without ever seeing a man lead out in Sabbath School."

Then she asked me to lead.

"Me? A cradle roll leader? I...I can't sing!" was my remembered protest.

But I did it.

OK, mothers didn't ask for my autograph and the pastor didn't award me a medal. But the rewards were there. Their names were Sally, Devon, Chris, Lori...

Truly "no man stands so tall as when he stoops to help a child."

—Kermit Netteburg

Resources

Fraley, Darrell. "Getting Men on Your Children's Ministries Team." Children's and Family Ministries booklet.

Roehlkepartain, Jolene. *Children's Ministry That Works!* Group Publishing, 1991.

Seeders, Lisa. "Six Ways to Encourage Volunteers." *Kid's Stuff,* Apr.-June 1997.

Senter. Mark III. *Recruiting Volunteers in the Church..* Victor Books, 1990.

Appendix A

Where to Order Materials

Adventist Book Centers
Go to www.adventistbookcenter.com or call 1-800-765-6955 to order. More than 60 ABC's serve the ministry needs of children's ministry leaders.

Advent*Source*
5040 Prescott Avenue
Lincoln, NE 68506
www.adventsource.org
Orders 1-800-328-0525
FAX 1-402-486-2572
Provides free catalogs for Children's Ministries, Pathfinder & Adventurer Ministries.

Christian Record Services, Inc.
P.O. Box 6097
Lincoln, NE 68506
www.christianrecord.org
Phone (402) 488-0981
FAX (402) 488-7582
TDD: (402) 488-1902
Provides materials, services and assistance for ministries to persons who are blind or hearing impaired.

Health Connection
55 West Oak Ridge Drive
Hagerstown, MD 21740
www.adventistwellness.org
Orders 1-800-548-8700
FAX (301) 790-9733

Free catalog with many programs, videos and visual aids for Health Ministries.

Pacific Press Publishing Association
1350 North Kings Road
Nampa, ID 83687-3186
www.pacificpress.com
Phone (208) 465-2500
FAX (208) 465-2531

Publisher of Children's Ministries magazines and books.

Review and Herald Publishing Association
55 West Oak Ridge Drive
Hagerstown, MD 21740
www.reviewandherald.com
Phone (301) 791-7000
FAX (301) 791-7012

Publisher of Children's Ministries magazines and books.

Appendix B

Planning a Children's Ministry Budget

Year _____

Sabbath School:

1.   Publishing House Materials

       Review & Herald   _____

       Pacific Press   _____

       Advent*Source*   _____

       Other _____   _____

2.   Division Operation

       Beginners   _____

       Kindergarten   _____

       Primary   _____

       Juniors   _____

       Earliteens   _____

3.   Equipment or Major Additions

       _____

       _____

Children's Ministries Outreach Activities:

    Vacation Bible School   _____

    Children's Evangelistic Meetings   _____

    Neighborhood Bible Clubs   _____

    Other _____   _____

Children's Ministries Nurture Activities

    Weekly Church Bulletins   _____

    Children's Newsletter   _____

    Baptismal Classes   _____

    Adventurer Club   _____

    Pathfinder Club   _____

    Other _____   _____

Miscellaneous

    _____   _____

    _____   _____

    _____   _____

TOTAL Children's Ministries Budget

    Sabbath School   _____

    Outreach Activities   _____

    Nurture Activities   _____

    Miscellaneous   _____

    TOTAL BUDGET   _____

52 Easy Program Ideas for Kindergarten Sabbath School
Robert Robinson

52 Easy Program Ideas is packed full of simple, effective and fun suggestions to accompany the *GraceLink Kindergarten Leaders/Teachers* guide. These creative new options will involve all the children in your class! No more cutting out millions of fall leaves or searching for fun crafts to illustrate the lesson—everything is here! Ideas include...room decorations, bulletin board suggestions, learning center instructions, simple memory verse songs, creative snack ideas, interactive Bible story ideas, patterns, recipes and much more!

Year A Program Ideas Book	**Catalog #021985**	**$12.95**
Year A Memory Verse CD	**Catalog #020032**	**$9.95**
Year B Program Ideas Book	**Catalog #021986**	**$12.95**
Year B Memory Verse CD	**Catalog #021984**	**$9.95**

To order call Advent*Source* at 800-328-0525 or www.adventsource.org.

Creative Bible Learning Activites for Primary

Noelene Johnsson and Trudy Morgan-Cole

We've all heard that many children learn and participate better if they can be actively involved. But finding new ways to keep their minds and hands busy isn't always easy! A brand new book from Advent*Source* is out with hundreds of Bible based activities that aren't just busy-work. These crafts, games and activities for Primary age children were created with learning in mind.

These creative options will help each child remember what they've learned. Every activity includes suggestions to plug into one or more GraceLink Sabbath School lessons. Use the comprehensive index to find specific activities recommended for next week's lesson—or choose and adapt any activity.

Ideas include:

Room decorations, Bulletin board suggestions, Art and crafts, Creative writing, Drama activities, Experiments, Experiential learning, Games and puzzles, and much more!

Catalog #021120 $14.95

To order call Advent*Source* at 800-328-0525 or www.adventsource.org.

Creative Bible Learning Activities
Fred & Kelly Blue Cornforth

You have the opportunity to motivate and challenge your junior teens to get excited about Christianity. With your help, junior teens can internalize sound Christian principles, and that's an awesome responsibility.

For years, leaders have been struggling with the question "How do we pass on our faith to future generations?" Recent research has shown that junior teens understand more and remember longer principles they discover for themselves. This understanding is the basis for *Creative Bible Learning Activities for Your Junior Teens*.

Filled with hope, encouragement, and practical advice, this book offers eight clues to understanding the special characteristics of junior teens and the struggles they face. Fred and Kelly Blue Cornforth present 101 creative Bible learning methods that will engage the participants in actively assessing their own spiritual journey. But *Creative Bible Learning Activities* doesn't just stop there. These learning activities also propel junior teens toward on-going, independent Bible study and discovery. A continuous journey of personal growth and discovery. That's the best kind of learning!

Catalog #021119   **$12.95**

To order call Advent*Source* at 800-328-0525 or www.adventsource.org.

The Colors of Grace In Our Homes
Stuart Tyner

Project Affirmation and the Valuegenesis task force clearly states that the children and youth in the Seventh-day Adventist church need to understand the value of the grace of Jesus Christ in their daily life. The question many parents have asked following these reports is: "How do I teach grace?"

Now there is an answer: *The Colors Of Grace In Our Homes*!

In this book, Stuart Tyner gives practical, down-to-earth suggestions on how to integrate grace into the home. Complete with 100 creative ways to experience and teach grace, this resource is ideal for parents that are leading their children and teens towards a higher level of faith maturity.

Learn how to:
- Establish a grace orientation in your home
- Discover the joy of worship
- Create a faith community within your family
- Encourage your children to live a life of service
- Sense God's presence in family worship

This book is just one of three in our Grace series. The other books are The Textures Of Grace In Our Schools and *The Sounds Of Grace In Our Churches*. Order separately or the complete series!

Catalog #602055 $8.95

To order call Advent*Source* at 800-328-0525 or www.adventsource.org.

The Sounds of Grace In Our Churches

V. Bailey Gillespie

Project Affirmation and the Valuegenesis task force clearly states that the children and youth in the Seventh-day Adventist church need to understand the value of the grace of Jesus Christ in their daily life. The question many church leaders have asked following these reports is: "How do I teach grace?"

Now there is an answer: *The Sounds Of Grace In Our Churches!*

In this book, V. Bailey Gillespie gives practical, down-to-earth suggestions on how to integrate grace into the church. Complete with 100 creative ways to experience and teach grace, this resource is ideal for church leaders who are leading their church's young people towards a higher level of faith maturity.

Learn how to:

- Establish a grace orientation in church
- Discover the joy of worship
- Create a faith community within your church family
- Encourage the children to live a life of service
- Sense God's presence in worship

This book is just one of three in our *Grace* series. The other books are *The Textures Of Grace In Our Schools* and *The Colors Of Grace In Our Homes*. Order separately or the complete series!

Catalog #602065   **$8.95**

To order call Advent*Source* at 800-328-0525 or www.adventsource.org.

180